THE ETHICS OF SOCIAL PUNISHMENT

How do we punish others socially, and should we do so? In her 2018 Descartes Lectures for Tilburg University, Linda Radzik explores the informal methods ordinary people use to enforce moral norms, such as telling people off, boycotting businesses, and publicly shaming wrong-doers on social media. Over three lectures, Radzik develops an account of what social punishment is, why it is sometimes permissible, and when it must be withheld. She argues that the proper aim of social punishment is to put moral pressure on wrongdoers to make amends. Yet the permissibility of applying such pressure turns on the tension between individual desert and social good, as well as the possession of an authority to punish. Responses from Christopher Bennett, George Sher, and Glen Pettigrove challenge Radzik's account of social punishment while also offering alternative perspectives on the possible meanings of our responses to wrongdoing. Radzik replies in the closing essay.

LINDA RADZIK is Professor of Philosophy at Texas A&M University. She is the author of *Making Amends: Atonement in Morality, Law and Politics* (2009), as well as a series of articles on the normative issues that arise in the aftermath of wrongdoing.

T0371060

THE ETHICS OF SOCIAL PUNISHMENT

PUNISHMENT

The Enforcement of Morality in Everyday Life

LINDA RADZIK

Texas A&M University

with
CHRISTOPHER BENNETT

University of Sheffield

GLEN PETTIGROVE

University of Glasgow

GEORGE SHER

Rice University

CAMBRIDGE
UNIVERSITY PRESS

CAMBRIDGE
UNIVERSITY PRESS

University Printing House, Cambridge CB2 8BS, United Kingdom

One Liberty Plaza, 20th Floor, New York, NY 10006, USA

477 Williamstown Road, Port Melbourne, VIC 3207, Australia

314–321, 3rd Floor, Plot 3, Splendor Forum, Jasola District Centre, New Delhi – 110025, India

79 Anson Road, #06-04/06, Singapore 079906

Cambridge University Press is part of the University of Cambridge.

It furthers the University's mission by disseminating knowledge in the pursuit of education, learning, and research at the highest international levels of excellence.

www.cambridge.org
Information on this title: www.cambridge.org/9781108836067
DOI: 10.1017/9781108870665

First published 2020

A catalogue record for this publication is available from the British Library.

Library of Congress Cataloging-in-Publication Data
Names: Radzik, Linda, 1970- author.
TITLE: The ethics of social punishment : the enforcement of morality in everyday life / Linda Radzik, with Christopher Bennett, George Sher, Glen Pettigrove.
DESCRIPTION: Cambridge, United Kingdom ; New York, NY : Cambridge University Press, 2020. | Includes bibliographical references and index.
IDENTIFIERS: LCCN 2020014767 (print) | LCCN 2020014768 (ebook) | ISBN 9781108836067 (hardback) | ISBN 9781108799294 (paperback) | ISBN 9781108870665 (epub)
SUBJECTS: LCSH: Social acceptance–Moral and ethical aspects. | Social isolation. | Punishment–Social aspects. | Judgment (Ethics)
CLASSIFICATION: LCC HM1111 .R33 2020 (print) | LCC HM1111 (ebook) | DDC 302/.14–dc23
LC record available at https://lccn.loc.gov/2020014767
LC ebook record available at https://lccn.loc.gov/2020014768

ISBN 978-1-108-83606-7 Hardback
ISBN 978-1-108-79929-4 Paperback

For Bob

Contents

vii

Notes on Contributors

LINDA RADZIK is Professor of Philosophy at Texas A&M University. She is the author of *Making Amends: Atonement in Morality, Law and Politics* (2009), as well as a series of articles on the normative issues that arise in the aftermath of wrongdoing.

CHRISTOPHER BENNETT is a Professor in the Philosophy Department at the University of Sheffield. He is the author of *The Apology Ritual: A Philosophical Theory of Punishment* (Cambridge 2008), as well as numerous articles in moral, political and legal philosophy. Among other things, he is currently working on expressive action and normative powers.

GLEN PETTIGROVE holds the Chair in Moral Philosophy at the University of Glasgow. He is the author of *Forgiveness and Love* (2012) and numerous articles in academic journals, including *Ethics, Nous, Philosophy and Phenomenological Research*, and the *Australasian Journal of Philosophy*.

GEORGE SHER is the Herbert S. Autrey Professor of Philosophy at Rice University, where he has taught since 1991. Before coming to Rice, he taught first at Fairleigh Dickinson University and then at the University of Vermont. His research interests range over topics in ethics, political philosophy, and moral psychology. He has edited or coedited a number of anthologies and is the author of seven books, including *Desert* (1987), *Beyond Neutrality: Perfectionism and Politics* (1997), *In Praise of Blame* (2006), and *Equality for Inegalitarians* (Cambridge University Press, 2014). His most recent project is a book on freedom of mind entitled *A Wild West of the Mind*.

Preface

The theme of my research for many years now has been the aftermath of wrongdoing and the moral decisions faced at those times by victims, wrongdoers, and third-party witnesses. What should we do after things have already gone wrong? I have studied these issues in legal and political contexts. But I am especially drawn to questions about the aftermath of wrongdoing in everyday life. What are morally appropriate responses to deceptions and betrayals among friends and family, or bullying in schools and workplaces, or racism and other forms of nastiness among neighbors, strangers on the street, or strangers on the Internet?

Sometimes, in cases like these, victims and witnesses tell the wrongdoers off, give them the cold shoulder, talk about them behind their backs, or even denounce them publicly on social media. Sometimes victims and witnesses to wrongdoing do nothing, of course; and sometimes they do nothing *for moral reasons*, believing it would be wrong to act. In recent years, I have written papers reflecting on each of these modes of response to wrongdoing: gossiping, boycotting, overtly criticizing, socially avoiding, and minding your own business. What I discovered was a surprising amount of complexity. Gossiping, boycotting, criticizing, avoiding, and minding one's own business simply do not hold together very well as action-types. The meanings and functions of token actions within these types vary widely. So, the considerations that seem relevant to justifying any particular instance of gossiping, boycotting, and so on vary widely as well. I have become convinced that I need a new strategy for thinking through these issues.

One theme that has cropped up continually in my research is punishment. Some instances of gossip seem to be punitive, although most are not. Some consumer boycotts look like attempts to punish wrongdoing businesses, although others seem to have different functions altogether, such as the avoidance of complicity. Sometimes we emotionally withdraw from friends and family members who have mistreated us in order to punish them, but at other times we do so simply for the sake of our own health and happiness.

This volume makes social punishment the central category of analysis. The philosophical literature on punishment is so wholly concentrated on the state's responses to crime that authors sometimes dismiss talk of punishment in everyday life as merely metaphorical. But this is mistaken. Legal norms are not the only ones that society enforces, and the mechanisms of law are not the only methods of enforcement that society uses. Chapter 1 defends a definition of punishment that can recognize and shed light on nonstate forms of punishment. Chapter 2 develops an account of what justifies using social punishment against another person that I call the "moral pressure theory." Chapter 3 considers a broad variety of ways in which social punishment can go wrong and proposes a set of ethical principles for limiting socially punitive behavior.

The invitation from the Tilburg Center for Moral Philosophy, Epistemology and Philosophy of Science (TiLPS) to deliver the Descartes Lectures in 2018 presented the perfect opportunity to organize my thoughts about punishment in everyday life. In December of that year, TiLPS hosted a conference on this theme, which included contributions from a talented and generous group of scholars. The Center also invited three philosophers whose work I have admired for years to respond directly to my lectures: Christopher Bennett, George Sher, and Glen Pettigrove. Their essays and my response are included in this volume.

In Chapter 4, Bennett both critiques my definition of punishment and offers a genealogical account of social responses to wrongdoing that points toward an alternative interpretation of the meaning and role of social punishment. Sher puts pressure on my theory of justification in Chapter 5, including both the desert condition and the instrumental condition that form the two halves of the moral pressure theory of punishment. In Chapter 6, Pettigrove offers an alternative lens for interpreting some of the phenomena that I classify as social punishment. Along the way, he develops a theory of protest as a response to wrongdoing. Each of these contributions leads me to alter and, I hope, improve my account of social punishment in some way, as I explain in Chapter 7.

I would like to express my most sincere and grateful appreciation to TiLPS, the Department of Philosophy at Tilburg University, and the organizers of the Descartes Lectures: Alfred Archer, Amanda Cawston, Bart Engelen, and Maureen Sie. This series of lectures builds on many years of research that has, at different times, received financial support from the Alexander von Humboldt Foundation, the Social Philosophy &

Policy Foundation, the Liberty Fund, the Glasscock Center for Humanities Research, and the Vice President for Research's Office at Texas A&M University. Thanks are also due to the participants at the conference associated with the Descartes Lectures, especially Christopher Bennett, Leonhard Menges, Per-Erik Milam, Paul Christopher Morrow, Glen Pettigrove, George Sher, Elise Springer, and Frank Wu. For their comments on various versions of this material, I would like to thank D. Justin Coates, Andrew I. Cohen, Douglas Husak, Luke Jonathan Maring, Dale E. Miller, Colleen M. Murphy, David Schmidtz, Timothy Schroeder, and Tamler Sommers. Thank you to my daughter, Mary Shandley, for her support for this project and her help interpreting the world of social media. This volume is dedicated to my husband, Robert R. Shandley, who always has a patient ear when I need one. He makes everything in my life better, including my writing.

PART I

The Descartes Lectures 2018

CHAPTER I

Defining Social Punishment

Linda Radzik

I INTRODUCTION

The term 'social punishment' is intended to distinguish our topic from legal punishment. As a first pass, we can think of social punishment simply as nonlegal (and nondivine) punishment. Examples of nonlegal punishments that readily pop to mind include parents grounding children, teachers giving students detention, or employers demoting employees. Each of these is an example of what I call *formal* social punishment. Parents, teachers, and employers act within fairly well-defined, hierarchically structured, institutional roles. In that way, the social punishments of parents and teachers resemble the legal punishments of judges and juries.

The sort of punishment that most interests me here is instead *informal social punishment*, or what Leo Zaibert calls "pre-institutional punishment."[1] It is what John Stuart Mill, in *On Liberty*, describes as the "moral coercion of public opinion."[2] These sorts of penalties are imposed by "public opinion" or "society" or one's "fellow-creatures," rather than by any sort of formal authority figure acting in an official capacity.[3] Mill's examples of informal social punishments include "depreciatory remark[s]," "disparaging speeches," sarcasm, and "vituperation," as well as shunning behaviors.[4]

Mill is one of the few philosophers who have addressed informal social punishment at any length.[5] He takes these sanctions quite seriously. In *On Liberty*, he writes,

---

[1] Leo Zaibert, *Punishment and Retribution* (New York: Routledge, 2006), 21–23.

[2] John Stuart Mill, *On Liberty*, in *Collected Works of John Stuart Mill*, vol. 18, ed. J. M. Robson (Toronto: University of Toronto Press, 1977), I.9. Citations of Mill's works specify chapter and paragraph number.

[3] Ibid., e.g., I.9 and I.11.

[4] Ibid., III.14, II.44, and III.6.

[5] Other examples include Zaibert, *Punishment and Retribution*; Ferdinand David Schoeman, *Privacy and Social Freedom* (New York: Cambridge University Press University Press, 1992); and William

3

Society can and does execute its own mandates: and if it issues wrong mandates instead of right, or any mandates at all in things with which it ought not to meddle, it practises a social tyranny more formidable than many kinds of political oppression, since, though not usually upheld by such extreme penalties, it leaves fewer means of escape, penetrating much more deeply into the details of life, and enslaving the soul itself.[6]

Readers who are familiar with Mill's biography cannot help but imagine that these words draw on his own, and his beloved Harriet Taylor's, painful experiences as the objects of gossip and scandal. Mill speculated that for historical and political reasons his society might have been particularly prone to using public opinion as a form of punishment.[7] But I wonder whether even Victorian England can compare with the call-out culture of Twitter in terms of sheer, soul-crushing power.

On the very day I delivered the first of these Descartes Lectures, my morning paper included a vivid example. A recent, online trend in the United States involves posting videos of people in the throes of drug overdoses.[8] Sometimes these videos are recorded and shared by police officers, with the apparent motive of drawing attention to the severity of the opioid epidemic in the United States and the need for some sort of action. Other videos appear to be posted by bystanders for the purposes of publicly shaming drug abusers. The videos frequently go viral, especially those in which parents have collapsed in front of their young children. Such videos typically generate both outrage and mockery, although some viewers instead reach out with encouragement or offers of aid. For some overdose victims, "the public shaming was a new way to hit bottom" in the sense that it created a moment of crisis that led them to seek treatment.[9] But for others, having one of the worst moments of their lives permanently archived on the Internet, available for viewing by family and coworkers as well as strangers, is an obstacle to recovery.

It is worth nothing that, while Mill is keenly aware of the dangers of ordinary people policing one another's behaviors, he does not categorically reject informal social punishment. Indeed, Mill writes in On Liberty, "If any one does an act hurtful to others, there is a prima facie case for

---

A. Edmundson, "Civility as Political Constraint," *Res Publica* 8, no. 3 (2002): 217–29. Also notable is historian Michael Cook's *Commanding Right and Forbidding Wrong in Islamic Thought* (New York: Cambridge University Press, 2000).

[6] Mill, *On Liberty*, I.5.
[7] Ibid., I.8.
[8] Katharine Q. Seelye, Julie Turkewitz, Jacky Healy, and Alan Blinder, "How Do You Recover after Millions Have Watched You Overdose?," *New York Times*, online edition, Dec. 11, 2018.
[9] Ibid.

punishing him, by law, or, where legal penalties are not safely applicable, by general disapprobation."[10] He expresses this thought even more strongly in *Utilitarianism*, saying that "we should be gratified" whenever injustices that fall outside the reach of the law are punished through social sanctions.[11] So, while Mill provides a clear case against socially punishing those who harm only themselves (e.g., by overdosing), he appears to support the social punishment of those who harm others (e.g., by neglecting and traumatizing their children).

I have very mixed feelings about punishment myself. I am deeply skeptical about the justification and effectiveness of criminal punishment in legal contexts. I rarely used punishment as a parent. But in this book, I argue that informal social punishment is permissible in some contexts. My goal is not to encourage informal social punishment but to bring attention to the fact that it goes on around us all the time and to develop tools for thinking critically about it.

In this first chapter, I take up the task of defining informal social punishment more clearly. Formulating a definition helps us distinguish social punishment from a range of other possible responses to wrongdoers, including blaming, morally criticizing, persuading, and minding one's own business.[12] Chapter 2 addresses the problem of justifying informal social punishment. Taking traditional debates about criminal punishment as my model, I ask what the general justifying aim of social punishment might be. Is it to dole out just deserts? To deter wrongdoing? To express or communicate some sort of message? I argue that none of the usual answers is quite right and develop an alternative. I have titled Chapter 3 "Practicing Social Punishment." Even when we grant that informal social punishment is justifiable in principle, justifying particular acts of punishment presents further difficulties.

Each of the three chapters highlights a different set of social practices that, I argue, are frequently used as informal social punishments. In this chapter, my main examples involve rebuking or pointedly socially avoiding wrongdoers. Chapter 2 features a consumer boycott of an unjust business. The third chapter focuses on the phenomenon of naming and shaming on social media, including the use of public shaming by the #MeToo campaign against sexual abuse and harassment and the #LivingWhileBlack

---

[10] Mill, *On Liberty*, I.11.
[11] John Stuart Mill, *Utilitarianism*, in *Collected Works of John Stuart Mill*, vol. X, ed. J. M. Robson (Toronto: University of Toronto Press, 1969), V.13.
[12] Unless otherwise indicated, I use the terms 'wrongdoer' and 'wrongdoing' to imply culpability.

campaign, which responds to the harassment and oversurveillance of
African Americans in everyday life.

Let's turn, then, to the task of defining informal social punishment more
precisely. You might well wonder whether this is really necessary. Philosophers in the analytic tradition have been known to fetishize definitions.
Analyzing a commonly used word like 'punishment' into necessary and
sufficient conditions and then using those conditions to sort hugely
complex sets of phenomena will inevitably feel artificial at times. We
should expect there to be marginal cases and reasonable disagreement.
Still, a good definition helps us coordinate our attention on a topic. It gives
us insights into that topic and helps us understand why controversial cases
are controversial. We should pay attention to what the definition leaves
out and consider whether it encourages us to make value-laden assumptions that should instead be interrogated. But if we keep these guidelines in
mind, definitions are helpful things.

The philosophical literature on punishment includes quite a bit of
debate about how punishment should be defined. It is remarkable just
how fully focused this literature is on legal punishment.[13] To give just one
example, David Boonin's 2008 book *The Problem of Punishment* is, despite
the title, solely concerned with legal punishment.[14] He simply ignores the
possibility of nonlegal punishment. I am picking on Boonin a bit here, but
he is hardly alone. Other authors mention that there are nonlegal kinds
of punishment and *then* ignore them, often dismissing them as "sub-
standard" or "secondary" cases.[15] Some, however, explicitly argue that
there is no such thing as nonlegal punishment. They dismiss talk of divine
punishment or parental punishment as either misuses of the term or mere
metaphors.[16] They certainly would not countenance the category of
informal social punishment. Arguments for denying the possibility of
nonlegal or informal punishments emerge in what follows. But I would

[13] For a thorough review of the literature on this point, see Zaibert, *Punishment and Retribution*, ch. 1.
[14] David Boonin, *The Problem of Punishment* (New York: Cambridge University Press, 2008). Leo
Zaibert makes this criticism of Boonin in "Punishment, Restitution, and the Marvelous Method of
Directing the Intention." *Criminal Justice Ethics* 29, no. 1 (2010): 41–53, at 42.
[15] H. L. A. Hart, "Prolegomenon to the Principles of Punishment," in *Punishment and Responsibility:
Essays in the Philosophy of Law*, 2nd ed. (New York: Oxford University Press, 2008), 1–27; and
Antony Flew, "The Justification of Punishment," *Philosophy* 29, no. 111 (1954): 291–307.
[16] Stanley I. Benn, "Punishment," in *The Encyclopedia of Philosophy*, vol. 7, ed. Paul Williams (New
York: Macmillan, 1967), 29–36.

like to register a few initial objections to the view that 'punishment' simple *means* legal punishment.

First, the practice of using words like 'punishment' in various languages for the actions of God and parents as well as kings and magistrates goes way back. Second, as Zaibert points out, many writers in the literature on criminal punishment (including Boonin) reason from premises about nonlegal forms of punishment to conclusions about legal punishment.[17] Third, ordinary, contemporary usage is on my side. People use the language of punishment to talk about nonlegal and informal types of penalties.

I have pulled just a few examples from my favorite advice columnist, Carolyn Hax of the *Washington Post*. (Yes, I have a favorite advice columnist. Advice columns are filled with discourse about everyday sorts of wrongdoing.)

- One letter writer says that her self-absorbed in-laws have never shown any interest in her as a person. She is hurt and angry and finds herself wanting to keep them from seeing the new grandchild. Hax suggests some possible reasons for her in-laws' behavior and then writes, "Now think of these possibilities and ask yourself, is any of these violations of character or behavior serious enough to warrant the punishment of losing their grandkids?"[18]
- Another woman confesses that she lied about seeing her brother's girlfriend cheating on him with another man. The lie was motivated by jealousy at how well the young couple are doing financially and professionally while the letter writer is still struggling. But she got caught in the lie and now her brother avoids being alone with her. Hax responds, "[I]f you seriously think your worst or only punishment . . . is that it's awkward right now and your main concern is wanting the awkward phase to pass faster . . ., then you have some more work to do with your conscience."[19] (I think Hax is implying here that the writer deserves both her brother's emotional withdrawal and the self-punishment of guilt and remorse.[20])

---

[17] Zaibert, "Punishment, Restitution, and the Marvelous Method of Directing the Intention," 43.
[18] Carolyn Hax, "'Strangers on a Train' Except with Carpooling Instead of Murder," *Washington Post*, online edition, May 25, 2018.
[19] Carolyn Hax, "Boom Chicka Pop to That," *Washington Post*, online edition, Oct. 26, 2017.
[20] Self-punishment is another morally rich phenomenon that tends to be overlooked when we define punishment to mean only "legal punishment."

- A third letter writer recounts having cheerily asked a co-worker, Polly, how her holiday was. In return, "[Polly] glared at [him] and stomped away." A year later Polly is still emotionally distant. It turns out that Polly had suffered a traumatic miscarriage over the holiday and posted about it at length on Facebook. Hax responds, "You have zero obligation to be aware of what people post on social media.... So if Polly has distanced herself as a way to punish you for your *faux pas*, then Polly is in the wrong."[21]

Is punishment merely a metaphor in Hax's vocabulary? It does not seem to be. Her use of the word seems perfectly straightforward. It would be much odder were she to write, "Gee, I just don't see the connection between your in-laws hurting your feelings and you wanting to block them from cuddling their grandchild" or "What could Polly be up to? She's not a court of law!" It is also worth mentioning that other academic literatures, including psychology and economics, discuss informal, social forms of punishment without pausing over the use of the word 'punishment.'[22]

In the end, though, the best answer I can give to someone who objects that there is no such thing as informal social punishment is that the proof of the pudding is in the tasting. In these chapters, I take the theoretical apparatus that was developed by philosophers to think through the moral complexities of state punishment and apply it to the ethics of responding to wrongdoing among social peers. If this exercise is profitable – if it helps us engage in deeper, wiser forms of moral reflection – then that is the best defense I can give for claiming that I am not misusing the word 'punishment.'

Just one more caveat before we get down to the task of formulating a definition: it is difficult to separate the task of defining punishment from the task of justifying punishment. We certainly do not want all punishments to turn out as permissible by definition. But I think we are going to find that 'punishment' is a thick term – it has both descriptive and normative elements. So, a certain amount of reasonable disagreement about what should be included in the definition and what should instead be considered a question of justification is probably inevitable.

---

[21] Carolyn Hax, "Nicknaming Awesomeness," *Washington Post*, online edition, Sept. 8, 2017.
[22] See, for example, Francesco Guala, "Reciprocity: Weak or Strong? What Punishment Experiments Do (and Do Not) Demonstrate," *Behavioral and Brain Sciences* 35 (2012): 1–15; Fiery Cushman, "Punishment in Humans: From Intuitions to Institutions," *Philosophy Compass* 10, no. 2 (2015): 117–33; and Klaus Jaffe, "Evolution of Shame as an Adaptation to Social Punishment and Its Contribution to Social Cohesiveness," *Complexity* 14, no. 2 (2008): 46–52.

3 THE STANDARD DEFINITION OF PUNISHMENT

What is often called the standard definition of punishment in the literature is the Flew–Benn–Hart definition.[23] These three authors – Antony Flew, S. I. Benn, and H. L. A. Hart – present roughly the same definition, with minor differences in phrasing, in separate articles. All three versions of the definition include clauses referring to the actions of "officials" or violations of "legal rules," which ensure that only legal forms of punishment count as punishments under their definitions. Flew and Hart mention the possibility of nonlegal punishments before putting them aside, while Benn dismisses the possibility of nonlegal punishments altogether. Boonin also defends a version of the Flew–Benn–Hart definition in his book. As I have already mentioned, Boonin does not take up the question of whether there are nonlegal forms of punishment. For my purposes, though, what is interesting about Boonin's version of the Flew–Benn–Hart definition is that it does not include any clauses that explicitly limit punishment to legal contexts. His discussion is only about legal punishment, but the definition itself is much more inclusive. Or so I will argue.

Boonin defines punishment as *authorized, intentional, reprobative, retributive harming.*[24] Since I plan to use the word 'retributive' to refer to a different concept in Chapter 2, I substitute the word 'reactive' to refer to the concept he has in mind. With this change in place, punishment is defined as *authorized, intentional, reprobative, reactive harming.* We can clarify this definition by seeing how these five criteria are fulfilled in a paradigmatic case of legal punishment – a sentence of imprisonment set by a criminal court.

First, punishing is a case of *harming.* Being confined to prison is clearly harmful. The harm condition in the definition of punishment is expressed in various ways in the literature: what is imposed is characterized as suffering, evil, or pain but also as unpleasantness[25] or hard treatment.[26] Herbert Fingarette suggests that what really characterizes punishment is the humbling of the person's will by imposing something on her she would

---

[23] Flew, "The Justification of Punishment"; Benn, "Punishment"; and Hart "Prolegomenon." In this paragraph, I draw on Zaibert's discussion of the Flew–Benn–Hart definition in *Punishment and Retribution*, ch 1.

[24] Boonin, *The Problem of Punishment*, 1–36.

[25] Flew, "The Justification of Punishment," 293; Benn, "Punishment," 29; and Hart, "Prolegomenon," 4.

[26] Joel Feinberg, "The Expressive Function of Punishment," in *Doing and Deserving: Essays in the Theory of Responsibility* (Princeton: Princeton University Press, 1970), 95–118, at 95.

prefer not to experience.[27] To me, all of these sound like forms of harm, so I favor that term.

Second, to say that a punishment is *reactive* is to say both that it is a reaction to the perceived transgression of a rule and that it is applied to the person who is believed to have committed the transgression.[28] Again, this is well illustrated with the example of imprisonment. Confinement of a person acknowledged to be innocent is kidnapping, not punishment.

The third criterion in Boonin's definition of punishment specifies that the harming is *reprobative*. That is, the infliction of harm is meant to express disapproval of the one being punished. Imprisonment is clearly expressive in this way. Furthermore, this criterion helps explain why fines are punishments rather than just fees for engaging in particular behaviors.

Fourth, punishment is *intentional* harming. Imprisonment is a harm that is intentionally imposed on the prisoner. In contrast, a criminal who is accidentally trapped when the sheriff closes off a cave with a steel grate is not thereby punished.[29] The sheriff did not mean to harm the criminal by installing the grate. Intention requires both that the punisher *knows* that he is imposing a harm and that he is imposing that harm for the *purpose* of punishment, that is, in order to cause harm as a response to the transgression.[30] If the sheriff knowingly traps the criminal in the cave but does so in order to prevent him from testifying about the sheriff taking bribes, the confinement would once again fail to qualify as punishment under the standard definition.

Finally, to count as a punishment the harming act must be *authorized*. It must fall within the legitimate jurisdiction of the agent imposing the sanction. The authorization criterion captures the intuition that, for example, mob aggression against a criminal is properly viewed as assault rather than punishment. Even if the criminal has been convicted of the crime through a legitimate and fair process, the mob are not the ones authorized to impose a penalty. The authorization condition helps explain why labeling something as a punishment gives it at least an air of legitimacy. Particular acts of punishment may be unjustified. Whole

---

[27] Herbert Fingarette, "Punishment and Suffering," *Proceedings and Addresses of the American Philosophical Association* 50, no. 6 (1977): 499–525.

[28] Similarly, rewards are "reactive" in that they are responses to praiseworthy actions.

[29] The example is drawn from Mark Twain, *The Adventures of Tom Sawyer* (Mineola, NY: Dover Publications, 1994).

[30] Wider readings of the purpose of punishment – what Hart would call the general justifying aim of punishment – should not be included in the definition of punishment (Hart, "Prolegomenon"). To do so would prematurely close off debate about whether and why punishing is justified.

systems of punitive norms and practices may be unjustified. But punishments are the sorts of things that are at least potentially justifiable. The standard definition helps us unpack that intuition. 'Punishment' has an air of legitimacy that 'assault' does not because punishment involves an *authorized* party harming a purported transgressor as a response to the transgression.

4 THE STANDARD DEFINITION ACCOMMODATES FORMAL SOCIAL PUNISHMENT

These same five conditions (authorization, intention, reprobation, reaction, and harming) accommodate the category of formal social punishment. Recall our earlier example of parents grounding children. These actions can also be described as authorized, intentional, reprobative, reactive harming. The parents impose harm on the child by restricting her liberty. They impose this harm intentionally (i.e., knowingly and purposely) in response to the child's misbehavior, thereby expressing their disapproval of her transgression. And they are authorized to do so because of their role as her parents.

The rule violated by the child is not a legal rule but instead a rule of the household, a moral rule, or maybe even a rule of etiquette. But unless we assume from the beginning that the only possible form of punishment is legal punishment, then there is no reason to restrict the class of transgressions in our definition. When we ask whether a case of harming is a case of punishment, the kind of rule that has been violated does not matter as much as the claim that the one who is imposing the harm is authorized to respond to a violation of that rule by imposing harm.

Cases of employers demoting employees for violating company rules and teachers giving students detention for violating school rules also fit the standard definition. Here too we have examples of authorized, intentional, reprobative, reactive harming. So what I have called formal social punishments easily qualify as punishments under Boonin's version of the standard definition.

5 THE STANDARD DEFINITION ACCOMMODATES INFORMAL SOCIAL PUNISHMENT

Now, I want to argue that the standard definition also accommodates the category of *informal* social punishments. Remember, I am using the word 'informal' just to refer to cases that do not involve people who are acting in hierarchically structured institutional roles but who are instead social equals.[31] My strategy is just to establish that social equals can also engage in authorized, intentional, reprobative, reactive harming. If punishment is defined by these five criteria, as the standard definition suggests, then social equals can punish one another.

I will use examples of rebukes between friends, family members, or coworkers to help illustrate my argument. Revising our earlier examples from Carolyn Hax's advice column a bit, imagine the brother telling his sister off for lying about his girlfriend. Or imagine Polly saying, "I can't believe you are so insensitive to ask me about my holiday! How can you treat my miscarriage so lightly!" As I use the term, a rebuke is an overt expression of disapproval, through words or gestures, addressed to a perceived transgressor, that both attributes responsibility to her for a transgression and expresses some form of anger, such as resentment or indignation. What I want to argue next is that cases of rebuke, even when they are between peers or social equals, are often instances of punishment.

Notice that I say "often." I do not need claim that all rebukes between peers are punishments just as I do not have to claim that all demotions of employees by employers are punishments. Sometimes employees are demoted because it is the only alternative to their being laid off. That is not a punishment because it is not a response to a transgression and it does not express reprobation. So while demotions are typically punishments, they are not always punishments. Similarly, sometimes friends rebuke one another because they simply lose their composure (e.g., they cannot help but roll their eyes), not because they are intentionally responding to a transgression. Not all rebukes will fit Boonin's definition of punishment, but I want to argue that many of them do. Let's go through each of the five conditions.

5.1 The Harm Condition

Can rebukes among friends qualify as cases of authorized, intentional, reprobative, reactive harming? Characterizing rebukes as *harmful* seems fair

---

[31] Let me here acknowledge a significant worry that I will not pursue. People who are social equals in the sense that they are not hierarchically differentiated by their roles in specific, formal institutions such as schools or workplaces may yet be quite unequal in the forms of power or influence they wield. Factors of age, race, gender, education, popularity, and so forth, in particular social contexts, may leave some people more or less able to inflict or to withstand punishment. So, by focusing on punishment among social equals, as I use that term here, I am going to miss a lot of morally significant aspects of the phenomena I am addressing. I hope to address this shortfall in future work.

enough. Being directly faced with angry criticism is generally considered unpleasant. Many of the expressions we use to describe rebukes have a distinctly violent tone to them. We "chew people out," "lay into them," and "rake them over the coals." Anyone who does not think that being overtly addressed with anger is harmful should watch my dramatic reenactment of my recent conversation with the repairman who let himself and his crew into my house without permission while no one was home (twice).

Of course, anger does not have to be the only emotion that is communicated in a rebuke. You can rebuke a friend while also expressing affection or cracking a joke, but unless anger is part of what is communicated, I would hesitate to call it a rebuke. It might be a moral criticism. Following Elise Springer, we can think of moral criticisms as communications that call another person's attention to a moral concern.[32] Or we might instead characterize moral criticisms as also communicating the thought that the one addressed is blameworthy. But I would like to reserve the word 'rebuke' for criticisms that have a harder edge to them. A rebuke does not merely attribute negative responsibility or assert that the hearer could be legitimately resented for his actions. In rebuking someone, you also send the message that *you* are angry with him. You *subject* him to your anger. You *target* your anger *at* him.

David Shoemaker denies that the kind of harming involved in rebuking counts as punishment, since it is not a case of "depriving you of anything to which you would otherwise have rights" had you not committed the wrong.[33] Shoemaker continues, "You don't have a right, for example, to my being pleasant around you or my not getting upset with you.... So while I may rail and pout and bluster and cry and condemn," I do not thereby punish.[34] In other words, even if I harm you by railing and blustering at you, I do not punish you.

I mentioned earlier that some theorists deny that there is such a thing as social punishment. Shoemaker here provides us with one reason for holding that view. The preliminary examples I have offered of possible social punishments have been things like rebuking, naming and shaming on the Internet, and giving cold shoulders. All of these would fail to count as punishments for Shoemaker because they do not appear to harm people

---

[32] Elise Springer, *Communicating Moral Concern: An Ethics of Critical Responsiveness* (Cambridge, MA: MIT Press, 2013).
[33] David Shoemaker, "Blame and Punishment," in *Blame: Its Nature and Norms*, ed. D. Justin Coates and Neal A. Tognazzini (New York: Oxford University Press, 2013), 100–118, at 115.
[34] Ibid.

in ways that they have rights not to be harmed. They simply amount to *saying* certain kinds of things, and people can be presumed to have a right to speak their minds, or to *not doing things*, such as not engaging in friendly interactions with one's sister or coworker. Other examples of reactive harming in everyday life more obviously touch on rights, such as slapping or punching a wrongdoer, but physical violence is unlikely to be defensible *as punishment*. Social equals living in a functional state may be justified in using violence against one another as self-defense against violence but not as punishment. So, if Shoemaker is right that we have a case of punishing only when we have a case of harming that deprives one of what would otherwise be a right, then social punishment appears to be, at best, a negligible category.[35]

I suspect that a lot of readers will share Shoemaker's intuition. But I also suspect that this intuition is in part a product of the philosophical literature's intense focus on legal forms of punishment. In contrast, familiar examples of formal social punishments do not involve depriving people of what would otherwise be a right. A child does not have a moral or legal right to play video games. That sort of thing is always a matter of the parent's discretion. Yet the parent can still punish the child by taking away the PlayStation. Teachers never violate a child's legal or moral rights by talking to their parents about their classroom behavior, but when the teacher says, "Don't do that or I'll tell your parents," he is clearly threatening to punish the student.[36]

Another reason that I want to reject Shoemaker's claim that punishment must deprive you of something to which you have a right is that it seems to me to be a case of what Hart calls a "definitional stop."[37] Hart uses this term in the debate about consequentialist justifications of punishment. It looks like consequentialists have to conclude that it would be permissible to punish an innocent person, if punishing that person would maximize good consequences. Some consequentialists try to avoid this objection by arguing that if the person is innocent, then the action does not count as punishment. If we just define punishment as the harming of a *wrongdoer*,

---

[35] Elsewhere, I have defined social punishment as punishment that is both nonlegal and that uses "social" means of punishment, which I defined as means that are normally legally available to ordinary people. I have decided not include the latter stipulation here in order to better separate questions of definition from questions of justification.

[36] This last example is from Joel Feinberg, *Harm to Self: The Moral Limits of the Criminal Law*, vol. 3 (New York: Oxford University Press, 1989), p. 215.

[37] Hart "Prolegomenon," 5–6. See also Zaibert's discussion of definitional stops in *Punishment and Retribution*, ch. 1.

then the objection is blocked. Hart thought this was an abuse of the practice of formulating definitions. The definition, in effect, blocks critical reflection by distracting people from the fact that consequentialism might still recommend intentionally throwing an innocent person in jail; the theorist just would not label that as punishment.

Shoemaker's argument is, of course, much less pernicious, but it too seems to put a definitional stop on reflection. As we have seen, he writes, "You don't have a right, for example, to my being pleasant around you or my not getting upset with you.... So while I may rail and pout and bluster and cry and condemn," I do not thereby punish.[38] Of course, Shoemaker could have proceeded from here to a reflection on permissible versus impermissible forms of railing and pouting and blustering and crying and condemning, but he does not. In fact, almost no one does. There is a large philosophical literature on blame as a judgment or an attitude but very little on the ethics of overtly blaming people. Springer has an excellent book on moral criticism, but even she does not really explore the line between merely criticizing and "railing and blustering."[39] Zaibert speculates that the philosophical literature's equation of punishment with legal punishment has put a definitional stop on moral reflection about these kinds of harms.[40] They are not punishments, so they are not important enough to subject to moral evaluation.

For these reasons, I believe that we should stick with the simple version of the harm condition rather than Shoemaker's harm-that-would-other-wise-violate-rights condition. But I would like to emphasize that this still leaves the door open to concluding that informal social punishments sometimes or even typically touch on moral rights. We will consider that possibility when we discuss the aim of punishment. But I do not think we should take this position as part of the very definition of punishment.

5.2 *The Reaction, Reprobation, and Intention Conditions*

Having agreed that social equals are able to harm one another, we can quickly grant that they are able to harm one another in ways that are also reactive, reprobative, and intentional. These are the next three of Boonin's five criteria for punishment. Let's return to our example of the sister who

---

[38] Shoemaker, "Blame and Punishment," 115.
[39] Springer, *Communicating Moral Concern.*
[40] Zaibert, *Punishment and Retribution*, ch. 1.

fabricated a story about her brother's girlfriend. Suppose the brother angrily rebukes his sister for lying.

The rebuke is reactive in the sense defined earlier in that the brother takes himself to be responding to a perceived transgression (a lie, an attempt to sabotage his relationship) and directs that response at the person he alleges to have committed the transgression (his sister). Here, the transgression in question is a moral transgression, but, of course, people also rebuke one another for wearing ugly shirts or being offsides in a football match. Those might also turn out to be cases of informal social punishment. And this seems fine. Moral rules are not the only ones that people enforce in their social interactions. Going forward, though, my main interest will be in the punishment of moral transgressions.

The brother's rebuke is also reprobative in that he is expressing his disapprobation of his sister's behavior. Rebukes are probably reactive and reprobative by definition. If they were not reactive and reprobative, they would not be rebukes. This, too, seems true even when the transgression in question is not a moral transgression.

The brother's rebuke, in this version of the example, is also intentional. Not all rebukes are intentional, but many are. When the brother addresses angry words to his sister, when he tells her just how despicable her lie was, he knows that she will find this unpleasant. This is part of his point in telling her off. He wants her to feel bad. If she does not feel bad, if she remains cool and unmoved, then his purpose is frustrated.[41]

With just four of our five criteria of punishment in place, we are already in a position to see how the standard definition of punishment can help us distinguish between forms of harming among social equals that are punitive and those that are not. For example, a brother might place all sorts of emotional pressure on his sister. Perhaps he purposefully induces painful emotions in her so that she will loan him money. These actions would be coercive or manipulative but not punitive. His emotionally pressuring her is punitive only if he is intentionally inducing unpleasant emotions as a reprobative reaction to an alleged transgression of hers.

The first four criteria of punishment also help us to capture a distinction Mill draws in *On Liberty* between social sanctions and natural penalties.[42] As I have mentioned, Mill is willing to endorse some instances of informal

---

[41] Am I here claiming that the general justifying aim of punishment is retributive, that is, that the ultimate good being sought is the wrongdoer's suffering? No. The brother's purpose is to harm, but it does not follow that the reason for harming is that his sister's suffering is a good in itself. This distinction will be explored further in Chapter 2.
[42] Mill, *On Liberty*, IV.6.

social punishment, but he did not approve of socially punishing people for behaviors or vices that harm only themselves. For example, he did not endorse socially punishing someone who is ruining his health with drink or who is obstinate. This is an application of Mill's well-known Harm Principle.[43] Self-harming behavior should be left alone. It is not our business. But while we cannot permissibly punish the imprudent or obstinate person, we can avoid him. Mill writes,

[We] are not bound, for example, to seek his society; we have a right to avoid it (though not to parade the avoidance), for we have a right to choose the society most acceptable to us. We have a right, and it may be our duty, to caution others against him, if we think his example or conversation likely to have a pernicious effect on those with whom he associates. We may give others a preference over him in optional good offices, except those which tend to his improvement.[44]

Notice that when we socially avoid someone in these ways, we *are* harming him. Mill implies that by referring to these as "penalties."[45] People have an interest in social contact and cooperation. Withdrawing from contact and cooperation with them may well set back their interests. But even when we are harming – and knowingly harming – the heavy drinker or the obstinate man by withdrawing from him, we are not punishing him. These are simply "natural" penalties, which Mill describes as "inconveniences ... strictly inseparable from the unfavorable judgment of others."[46]

By appealing to the standard definition of punishment, we can say that what separates a social punishment from a natural penalty is the intentional, reprobative, reactive character of the harming. Mill says you are permitted to avoid the self-harming person but not to parade your avoidance. You can knowingly harm him, but you cannot purposefully harm him as a reprobative response to his actions or character. The purposeful expression of a message of disapproval turns social avoidance from a case of merely minding your own business to a case of social punishment.

Interestingly, Shoemaker suggests that rebukes are not punishments because the point of actively blaming someone is communicative rather than punitive. The function of overtly expressing blame, he writes, is to communicate to the wrongdoer a "basic moral demand, the claim we have

---

[43] "That principle is, that the sole end for which mankind are warranted, individually or collectively in interfering with the liberty of action of any of their number, is self-protection. That the only purpose for which power can be rightfully exercised over any member of a civilized community, against his will, is to prevent harm to others" (ibid., I.9).
[44] Ibid., IV.5.
[45] Ibid., IV.11.
[46] Ibid., IV.6.

on one another for goodwill (or at least no bad will)."[47] I find this a bit odd
because Shoemaker recognizes that punitive and communicative functions
are not necessarily incompatible. In fact, he notes that legal punishment "is
a kind of communication that is in actuality inseparable from the deliber-
ate causing of suffering constitutive of punishment in the first place."[48] In
contrast, Shoemaker describes any form of harm that attends "[a]nger,
remonstration and writing the other off" as purely incidental.[49] However,
I believe that the resemblance to legal punishment is much closer than
Shoemaker allows.

Calmly stating a moral claim, or attempting to persuade an offender
with a cool display of moral reasoning, is significantly different from
angrily confronting or coldly shunning that person. Rebukes and cold
shoulders send their moral message to the offender by knowingly and
purposefully subjecting him to hard treatment. In this way, the standard
definition of punishment also helps us to draw a distinction between
socially punishing and merely expressing blame. Overtly blaming is an
intentionally reprobative reaction to a transgression. It might even be
experienced as harmful by the target, who may feel exposed or humiliated.
But merely blaming does not intentionally (i.e., knowingly and purposely)
impose a harm. "I'm not saying this in order to hurt or upset you, but
I think you are in the wrong here," one might say. Such moral criticisms
are neither rebukes nor social punishments.

5.3 The Authorization Condition

This brings us to the fifth and final condition in Boonin's version of the
standard definition: authorization. The idea is that it is appropriate to
classify a form of harming as punishment only when it is meted out by
someone with a claim to authority over the transgression and the transgressor. Earlier I stipulated that informal social penalties are precisely those
sorts of penalties imposed by social equals, rather than by someone acting
from a position of authority within a hierarchical institution. So, the
authorization condition seems to present me with a problem. Both
Shoemaker and H. J. McCloskey accept the authorization criterion and
so deny that there is such a thing as informal social punishment.[50] No one

---

[47] Shoemaker, "Blame and Punishment," 117.
[48] Ibid.
[49] Ibid.
[50] Ibid., 114; and H. J. McCloskey, "The Complexity of the Concepts of Punishment," *Philosophy* 37,
no. 142 (1962): 307–25.

is "entitled to punish moral offenses *qua* moral offenses," writes McCloskey.[51] Meanwhile Zaibert, who is convinced that there are informal social punishments, concludes that he must reject the authorization condition in his definition of punishment.[52] But I want to have it both ways. I want to retain the authorization condition as part of the standard definition of punishment, and I want to argue that this condition can be satisfied in informal cases.

The secret to having it both ways is simply to deny that the authority in question must be asymmetrical. Legal punishment is marked by an asymmetrical form of authority, but this is because the forms of harm characteristic of legal punishments involve depriving people of things to which they would otherwise have a legal right. Physically confining a person or taking her property are things that people are typically both morally and legally prohibited from doing. So it seems appropriate to require that the authority to impose such penalties be reserved to a small number of people acting within formalized, public, and preferably democratically selected rules and institutions.

However, the harming acts that are typical responses to everyday wrongdoing are things such as delivering rebukes, pointedly avoiding someone, and encouraging people to join boycotts, which clearly do not violate (at least) *legal* rights. People do not need a hierarchical form of authority to do things like these. Those who rebuke and avoid wrongdoers are themselves subject to being rebuked and avoided by these very same people when they do wrong.

This is not to say that questions of authority are absent, however. To see this, think of cases of hypocrisy. Imagine that one friend rebukes the other for arriving half an hour late for a planned dinner. The first friend has been left sitting alone at a table in a restaurant, deflecting pressure from the waiter to either order or leave, and receiving pitying glances from the other diners, who assume she has been stood up. The rebuked friend replies, "You're one to talk! You are *constantly* late! If I had a nickel every time I was stuck somewhere waiting for you, I'd be a rich man!" Notice that the second friend's claim is not that he is not to blame for keeping his friend waiting or that rebuking a friend is never appropriate. He is saying that *she* is not entitled to be angry with him because of her own habitual lateness. A more punctual friend might well rebuke him, but she may not. She has lost her authority to do so through her own faults. But this, of course, implies that friends in general do have such authority.

[51] McCloskey, "The Complexity of the Concepts of Punishment," 310.
[52] Zaibert, *Punishment and Retribution*, 39.

Another set of cases that points to the phenomenon of authority are those in which the proper response to a rebuke is, "Mind your own business!" Imagine that a diner at a neighboring table delivers the rebuke to the late-arriving friend. "How rude to keep your friend waiting!" Once again, I think he would be justified in claiming that this stranger is not entitled to rebuke him. While it is true that he acted wrongly in keeping his friend waiting, the stranger lacks the authority to call him out for it. But in noticing these specific circumstances in which authority is lacking, we also are led to notice that authority can be present and that it can be held by people who are social equals of the wrongdoer. If the friend he kept waiting were herself reasonably punctual, she would have had the authority to rebuke him. And if he were to respond to a punctual friend's rebuke for keeping her waiting by saying, "Mind your own business!" then he would be making a rather shocking mistake.

The authority to punish is an interesting, complicated phenomenon. For example, I have appealed to your intuition that the neighboring diner lacks the standing to punish the late friend, but I have not explained why she lacks it. Chapter 3 will explore issues of authority in more depth. But for the moment, we have what we need. Remember, I do not have to argue that all rebukes among social equals meet the authorization condition and count as punishments but only that some do. I have argued that this is possible because the authority in question can be held mutually and symmetrically among peers. If this is so, then at least some rebukes among peers are cases of authorized, intentional, reprobative, reactive harming, and so there is such a thing as informal social punishment.

6 CONCLUSION AND MARGINAL CASES

My goal in this chapter has simply been to establish that there is a set of phenomena, common in our everyday lives, that amounts to an informal, nonlegal form of punishment. I have made this argument by appealing to Boonin's version of the standard, Flew–Benn–Hart definition of punishment: punishment is authorized, intentional, reprobative, reactive harming. I have argued that we find examples of precisely these sorts of actions in ordinary people's responses to transgressions committed by their peers. Informal social punishments are just nonlegal forms of authorized, intentional, reprobative, reactive harming between people who are not acting within hierarchically structured institutional roles but are instead social equals.

Earlier I noted that we should attend both to what definitions reveal and to what they lead us to ignore. So I would like to close this chapter on the definition of social punishment by highlighting some cases that may not fit our definition but that we may be tempted to label as punitive.

First, consider an ambiguity in the idea that punishment is reprobative. Does this mean that the harming act *expresses* reprobation or that it *communicates* reprobation? To my mind, the difference between mere expression and communication is the presence (or maybe the intended presence) of an audience to receive and comprehend the message. In legal cases of punishment, the reprobative element is public and far from subtle, so it is fair to describe it as communicative and to expect that the one being punished is part of the intended audience for that communication. But what should we say about cases of blacklisting, for example, which are often kept secret? When Hollywood producers of the 1950s kept secret lists of suspected communists and union organizers and refused to hire those people, were they punishing them? If we think of reprobative harming as harming that expresses reprobation, this looks like an example of punishment. But if we think that reprobative harming requires the communication of reprobation to an audience, and perhaps specifically to an audience that includes the one being punished, then secret punishments are not technically punishments. My own inclination is to conceive of the reprobative element as expressive rather than communicative, which means that more instances will come under the umbrella of social punishment, including some cases of gossip. However, when we move on to the problem of determining whether particular acts of social punishment are justified or not, secret punishments such as blacklisting and gossiping are likely to run into objections precisely because the reprobative message is not communicated to the target.

I would also like to pause here over the intention condition in our definition of punishment. Defining punishments as intentional forms of harming means, of course, that unintentional forms of harming do not count as punitive. However, when we look at the interactions of friends and family members in the aftermath of wrongdoing, we find many examples of what we might be tempted to call unconscious punishing. Recall Polly, from our earlier example, whose coworker cheerily asked about her holiday after she had just suffered a miscarriage. When she scowls and stomps out of the room, is she really punishing him? Probably, I think. I suspect that in the moment she was knowingly and purposefully sending him a nonverbal rebuke. The punishment was unfair (she should not have expected him to keep up with Facebook and so know about her miscarriage), but it looks like a punishment. When Polly continues to freeze him out a year after this incident, is she *still* punishing him? Maybe not. Perhaps she now recognizes that he did nothing wrong, but she still associates him with a terribly painful time in her life. Her long-term emotional withdrawal from him may not be an intentional form of reprobation or harming but might be an unintentional one. Perhaps she is still blaming him (unfairly) deep down for some of the pain she suffered without being aware that she is doing so.

Recall also the example of the woman who has felt disrespected by her in-laws for years and finds herself not wanting them to have contact with her new baby. Is she punishing them, as Hax suggests? She may instead think of herself as protecting her child from a relationship with people who will mistreat him. Which is it? Very likely the daughter-in-law herself will be unsure of her real intentions. I suspect that this kind of uncertainty is very common.

Notice also that the parents-in-law in the example might feel as though they are being punished even if the daughter-in-law's choice to keep them away from their grandchild does not count as a punishment under the standard definition. Suppose the daughter-in-law's sole purpose in denying them access is the welfare of her child. This would then count as a natural penalty of the grandparents' poor characters, not as a social punishment inflicted by their daughter-in-law. But the grandparents may suffer just as much, and the daughter-in-law may be fully aware that this will be the consequence of her choice.[53]

Similarly, penalties imposed by meddlers, like the one wherein the diner at a neighboring table rebukes a stranger for keeping his friend waiting, do not count as punishments because they do not meet the authorization condition. But they may yet be cases of unjustified intentional harming. Failing them to label them punishments may lead us to overlook or downplay their moral significance.[54]

Given the standard definition of punishment I have defended here, neither unconscious punishments nor natural penalties nor penalties inflicted by meddlers count as punishments. But I would like to flag them

---

[53] Roger Wertheimer reflects on the harmfulness of natural penalties (though he does not use this label) in "Constraining Condemning," *Ethics* 108, no. 3 (1998): 489–501. Wertheimer appears to conclude that cases of informal social punishment will be rare (at best) because the required forms of authority will rarely be held.

[54] Thanks to Douglas Husak for pointing out this way in which the threat of a definitional stop reemerges (personal communication). Husak suggests, quite reasonably, that the authorization condition may be better thought of as a condition of justification rather than definition. But I continue to treat it as a matter of definition, given the prominence of the standard definition.

as marginal cases. They are similar enough to punishments that we may benefit from thinking about them in the terms we use to think about punishment. Keeping in mind the moral worries that these marginal cases raise may also help us to think more clearly about the less marginal cases.

This, then, concludes the first step of the project. I have offered a definition of informal social punishment. In Chapter 2, we will turn to the question of what – if anything – can justify subjecting other people to such treatment. I hope to have established that this is a question worth asking. If I am correct, informal social punishment is not only a genuine phenomenon but quite a common one.

CHAPTER 2

Justifying Social Punishment

Linda Radzik

I INTRODUCTION

The goals of the last chapter were to clarify what social punishment is, to draw attention to the fact that it is a phenomenon in everyday life, and to suggest that it merits the attention of philosophers. The goal of this chapter is to ask whether social punishment – specifically, the *informal* social punishment of *moral* wrongdoing – is justifiable.[1] Is it ever permissible for ordinary people to punish one another for their moral transgressions? If so, why is this? What might be valuable or desirable about such forms of punishment?

As we turn from a discussion of what informal social punishment is to whether it can be justified, it will be helpful to have some examples at hand where the harm being imposed is more obvious than in the cases of rebuking friends or avoiding coworkers, which formed my main examples in Chapter 1. So, let's think of boycotts. Not all boycotts are punitive, but paradigmatic consumer boycotts often are.[2] Here, a group of private individuals voluntarily commit themselves to not buying a particular product in protest to some sort of transgression by that seller. Imagine consumers boycotting a chain of coffee shops, Joe's Coffee, because the company engages in exploitative scheduling practices.[3] They schedule and reschedule workers at the last moment, not allowing them enough notice to make proper childcare arrangements. They send workers who are paid by the hour home when business is slow, despite the fact that the workers

---

[1] Some passages in this chapter appear in previously published work, including "Moral Rebukes and Social Avoidance," *Journal of Value Inquiry* 48, no. 4 (2014): 643–61; and "Desert of What? On Murphy's Reluctant Retributivism," *Criminal Law and Philosophy* 11, no. 1 (2017): 161–73.

[2] See Linda Radzik, "Boycotts and the Social Enforcement of Justice," *Social Philosophy & Policy* 34, no. 1 (2017): 102–22.

[3] This is a fictionalized version of a real case. Since the real chain of coffee shops reportedly acted promptly to improve conditions for their workers, it struck me as inappropriate to use their name here.

have already invested money and effort in transportation and childcare in order to report to work. These practices are reported in the news, and, as a response, someone starts a hashtag, #BoycottJoesCoffee, which gains thousands of "likes" and reposts from people who resolve to buy their coffee elsewhere.

This case falls under the definition of punishment developed in Chapter 1. It is a case of intentional, reprobative, reactive harming. It also seems to meet the authorization condition, since how Joe's Coffee treats its workers is of legitimate interest to its customers. I must put off a full discussion of authority until the next chapter. But, for now, I simply appeal to the intuition that the customers are not failing to mind their own business in boycotting Joe's. So, this looks like a case of social punishing. It should be classified as an *informal* social punishing because the ones being punished (the coffee company, its owners and managers) and the ones doing the punishing (the group of consumers) are social equals. Neither one has any formal, hierarchical kind of authority over the other.

Notice that the harming that is distinctive of a consumer boycott includes both social avoidance and public rebuke. Boycotts are generally interpreted to be aggressive sorts of actions that convey moral anger. But, additionally, the consumers aim to harm Joe's Coffee by reducing its revenue and hurting its reputation.

I return to this example over the course of the chapter and ask whether and how a punitive boycott like this might be justified. My strategy is to ask what the "general justifying aim" of informal social punishment might be.[4] What overarching goal might the boycotters have that would provide a legitimate reason for intentionally harming their target in these ways? In posing the question in this form I am following the lead of generations of philosophers of law and their discussions of the justification of criminal punishment. In fact, almost all of the theories and writers I reference below originally concentrated on legal rather than social punishment. (I won't bother noting this as I go along. Just assume I'm taking them out of context!)

Part of my project here is to show how easily and fruitfully the philosophy of criminal punishment can be extended to informal social punishment, thereby bolstering my argument for thinking about things like rebukes and boycotts *as punishments*. But I also aim to develop and

[4] The phrase is due to H. L. A. Hart, "Prolegomenon to the Principles of Punishment," in *Punishment and Responsibility: Essays in the Philosophy of Law*, 2nd ed. (New York: Oxford University Press, 2008), 1–27, at 8.

defend a specific account of the general justifying aim of informal social punishment. The usual contenders in the debates about criminal punishment – retributivist, utilitarian, expressivist, and communicative theories – all encounter problems as accounts of informal social punishment.[5] I instead defend something I call the "moral pressure" account.

2 TYPES OF GENERAL JUSTIFYING AIMS

There are three strategies for identifying the general justifying aim of punishment: purely backward-looking, purely forward-looking, and mixed strategies. A purely backward-looking theory looks to a past, wrongful action to find the reasons for punishing. Typically, the goal of punishment is to deliver the wrongdoer's just deserts for that wrong. The wrongdoer's negative desert is said to provide both a necessary and a sufficient justification for punishment. The most prominent among this family of theories is the pure retributivist view, which holds that wrongdoers intrinsically deserve to suffer for their misdeeds.[6] Desert provides both the reason to punish and a limit on punishment. The suffering imposed should be proportional to – or, at least, not in excess of – either the blameworthiness of the wrongdoer or the wrongfulness of the action. Why should we, the consumers, boycott Joe's Coffee? Because they deserve to suffer for having mistreated their employees. How much suffering may we permissibly inflict on Joe's? As much as (but not more than) they culpably inflicted on their employees.

The standard objection to pure retributivism is that it is a repugnant, bloodthirsty view because it counts the suffering of other human beings as intrinsically desirable. The pure retributivist might emphasize that she only values the suffering of the guilty, but I hardly see how this helps. The suffering of the wrongdoer is portrayed as a good in itself, which justifies punishment even if punishing makes neither the victim, nor the wrongdoer, nor anyone else any better off.[7]

---

[5] I believe these theories also fail to justify criminal punishment, and typically for the same sorts of reasons as those I provide below. But I do not pursue that line of argument here.

[6] Different theorists use the label 'retributivism' to refer to different ideas. For some, it refers to purely desert-based justifications of punishment. Others apply the label to any partially desert-based theory. I use the term to refer only to the view that desert *of suffering*, specifically, is both necessary and sufficient for the justification of punishment.

[7] I took advantage of the invitation to Tilburg University to visit the Jheronimus Bosch Art Center in the nearby town of Den Bosch. The museum houses reproductions of the artist's paintings, as well as statues made by contemporary artists of various demons and monsters depicted in the paintings. Bosch's vision of hell is a playground of inventive cruelty. Sin in this life and spend eternity

In contrast, purely forward-looking strategies for justifying punishment appeal solely to the good consequences that can be achieved through punishing. A classic example of this approach is a utilitarian theory that appeals to the power of punishment to deter future wrongdoing. Why should we boycott Joe's Coffee? Because it might lead them and companies like them to end exploitative scheduling practices. Utilitarians count all suffering as bad but argue that the badness of one party's suffering (the company's) can be justified if it leads to a greater reduction in suffering overall (for the workers both at Joe's and elsewhere).

Purely forward-looking justifications of punishment also run into well-known problems. One is known as the "problem of innocents." Notice that the boycott might well deter wrongdoing even if the news story about Joe's Coffee is false – even if they have not mistreated their workers in the ways reported. A large boycott of Joe's still might lead other employers to improve their scheduling practices. If punishment is justified solely by its consequences, then there would still be sufficient reason to punish Joe's Coffee despite their innocence. But this is clearly objectionable, as it treats the owners and managers of Joe's Coffee as mere means to the well-being of other people. This is a fundamental denial of respect to them.

In light of these objections to the first two strategies for justifying punishment, most theorists turn to a mixed strategy: one that combines both backward- and forward-looking elements in the justification of punishment. For example, one might argue that punishment is justifiable only if (1) the one being punished is guilty and the penalty is proportional to the guilt *and* (2) punishment will deter future wrongdoing. This mixed strategy retains the desert element, which many see as "vital to our conception of ourselves and others as responsible beings."[8] But it also rejects intentionally harming wrongdoers when doing so is unlikely to bring about a better state of affairs in the future. In the case of Joe's Coffee, the boycott would be justified only if the company is guilty of mistreating their workers, only if the suffering imposed on them is proportionate to the misdeed, and only if the punishment is reasonably likely to lead to improvements. Views like this are sometimes described as "constrained

---

straddling a giant knife or being continually devoured and shat out again by a giant bird. My husband and I giggled our way through the collection, but it is sobering to reflect that these festivals of torture were believed to be a depiction of *justice* – justice on a pure retributivist model.

[8] Jeffrie G. Murphy, *Punishment and the Moral Emotions: Essays in Law, Morality, and Religion* (New York: Oxford University Press, 2012), 86.

instrumentalism," because the desert condition constrains the use of punishment as a means to pursuing good outcomes.[9]

In what follows, I pursue a mixed strategy. I argue that the general justifying aim of informal social punishment has both a desert-based element and an instrumental element. However, the theory I defend must be more complicated than the simple "guilt plus deterrence" model I just sketched. For one thing, I think respect for persons requires us to pursue a richer sort of good than mere deterrence. Second, I believe the desert condition needs to be reconceived in order to avoid the charge of blood-thirstiness. I reject the claim that what the guilty deserve is, specifically, suffering. In the next section, I examine some alternative ways of thinking about what is deserved by wrongdoers and how that kind of desert might provide reasons for punishment.

3 THE DESERT ELEMENT IN A CONSTRAINED INSTRUMENTALIST APPROACH

The key to retaining a desert element in a justification of punishment while avoiding the bloodthirsty suggestion that the suffering of another person is intrinsically valuable is to notice that "desert" need not mean "desert of suffering."[10] Desert is often analyzed as a three-part relation, in which someone (the subject) deserves something (the object) due to some fact about herself (the desert basis).[11] It is easy to come up with examples in which the place for the object is filled in with something other than suffering. A student deserves praise for her hard work. Here, praise is the object. An athlete deserves the opportunity to compete for the championship given his qualifying times in earlier races. In this example, the opportunity is the object. Desert can take many objects.

In discussions of punishment, it has seemed inevitable that the object of desert is suffering. After all, the topic at hand is the justification of *punishment* and punishing is, by definition, a form of harming. Harming, in turn, predictably brings suffering – a subjective experience of pain, evil, or unpleasantness. But it seems to me that there is a difference between the

---

[9] Victor Tadros, *The Ends of Harm: The Moral Foundations of Criminal Law* (New York: Oxford University Press, 2011).

[10] See also T. M. Scanlon, "Giving Desert Its Due," *Philosophical Explorations* 16, no. 2 (2013): 101–16; and Randolph Clarke, "Some Theses on Desert," *Philosophical Explorations* 16, no. 2 (2013): 153–64.

[11] Owen McLeod, "Desert," in *Stanford Encyclopedia of Philosophy*, ed. Edward N. Zalta (2008), plato.stanford.edu.

idea that one can deserve to be subjected to a harm and the idea that the thing deserved is, specifically, suffering. For example, if I win a free tattoo in a raffle, the object of desert is a prize, not suffering, even though this prize inevitably involves suffering. In the next part of the chapter, I examine several different ways of conceiving of the desert element that emerge in the literature on punishment. Each presents a different account of the object of desert in cases of wrongdoing.[12] The goal is to find a way of thinking about what wrongdoers deserve that is not bloodthirsty, that is, that does not suggest that what we intrinsically value is the suffering of the guilty as such.

3.1 Object of Desert: Expression of Reprobation

One suggestion is that the thing wrongdoers deserve is an expression of a negative moral judgment and disapprobation.[13] Punishment expresses reprobation. Indeed, reprobation is part of the standard definition of punishment, as we have seen. Expressivist justifications of punishment make the further claim that this expression of reprobation is the very thing that is deserved in the sense that it is intrinsically fitting to the culpable act. Punishing can therefore be justified on the grounds that it gives the wrongdoer what he deserves.

Some theorists defend this approach by arguing that wrongful actions have an expressive content to which punishment is a fitting reply.[14] For example, through their exploitative scheduling practices, the owners and managers of Joe's Coffee send the message that their employees' interests are not as worthy of consideration as their own and that they are not deserving of fair terms of employment. This message is false. In punishing Joe's Coffee, the boycotters offer a correction to the false claim. They send the message that Joe's employees are worthy of respectful treatment and that Joe's owners and managers are in the wrong.

In this way, expressivist defenses of punishment have the potential to avoid the bloodthirsty suggestion that what wrongdoers deserve is

---

[12] The theories of punishment that I will discuss do not generally describe themselves as presenting alternative objects of desert. More frequently, they take themselves to be interpreting what forms of suffering are deserved rather than arguing that something other than suffering is the object of desert.

[13] See, for example, Jean Hampton, "Correcting Harms versus Righting Wrongs: The Goal of Retribution," *UCLA Law Review* 39, no. 6 (1992): 1659–702. Note that some theories that describe themselves as expressivist are what I will label "communicative theories." See, for example, Bill Wringe, *An Expressive Theory of Punishment* (Basingstoke, UK: Palgrave Macmillan, 2016).

[14] Hampton, "Correcting Harms versus Righting Wrongs."

suffering. On this account, what they deserve is counterexpression. They deserve to have their false message met with a true one. Punishments like the boycott are just the means of expressing the true claim.

But critics question whether punishment can be justified simply as a form of fitting counterexpression. For one thing, one can express a true moral claim without addressing it *to the wrongdoer*. Joe's customers might simply utter their moral disapproval of Joe's to one another or tell the mistreated employees that they deserve better. To show that the expression of reprobation is fitting is not yet to show that the explicit targeting of that message at the wrongdoer is justified.

3.2 Object of Desert: Communication of Censure

For this reason, we might replace an expressivist account of desert with a communicative one.[15] Mere expression does not require an audience. Communication does. The main idea of a communicative theory of punishment is that the *wrongdoer*, specifically, deserves censure. The wrongdoer deserves to be directly addressed with message of condemnation, which is appropriate to his degree of culpability. Keep in mind here that this censure is meant to be justified on the grounds that it is intrinsically fitting. Censuring a wrongdoer might also have good consequences, such as deterrence, but for the moment we are interested in what the wrongdoer deserves. The answer given by communicative theories is that the wrongdoer intrinsically deserves censure.

Being targeted with censure is unpleasant. If the one censured fully grasps the truth of what is being communicated to him – namely, that he acted wrongly and is blameworthy for his action – then he will experience remorse, which is a painful emotion. So, censure involves suffering. But notice that the communicative theorist has room to argue that the wrongdoer's suffering is not itself the object of desert but merely a side effect of his getting what he does deserve, namely, censure. The communicative theorist need not value the wrongdoer's suffering qua suffering, and so the communicative theorist can escape the charge of bloodthirstiness.

However, one might well object that suffering is not merely a side effect of an appropriate moral communication, as suffering is the side effect of a tattoo. In cases of punishment, suffering is *the means by which the message is*

---

[15] See, for example, Andrew von Hirsch, *Censure and Sanctions* (New York: Oxford University Press, 1994); and R. A. Duff, *Punishment, Communication, and Community* (New York: Oxford University Press, 2001).

communicated. Joel Feinberg raises this objection in his classic article "The Expressive Function of Punishment." Throwing people in prison does send a message of condemnation, but surely we could send that message in a less violent manner. Feinberg writes, "One can imagine an elaborate public ritual, exploiting the most trustworthy devices of religion and mystery, music and drama, to express in the most solemn way the community's condemnation of a criminal for his dastardly deed."[16] "Perhaps this is only idle fantasy," Feinberg continues. "The only point I wish to make here is one about the nature of the question. The problem of justifying punishment, when it takes this form, may really be that of justifying our particular symbols of infamy."[17] In our example of Joe's Coffee, the boycotters do not simply write a letter or perform a play to communicate their censure. They intentionally damage Joe's reputation in the marketplace and reduce their revenue. What justifies sending their message by these means?[18]

3.3 Object of Desert: Communication of Negative Reactive Attitudes

One response to this objection is that one cannot communicate the appropriate message to the wrongdoer unless one communicates the angry reactive attitudes that the culpable action deserves. Simply sending Joe's Coffee a letter with a dispassionate, philosophical analysis of the injustice of their scheduling practices would fail to communicate all of what is fitting. It would not effectively convey the moral significance of the injustice nor the depth of the customers' concern and disapprobation. Joe's Coffee deserves to be targeted with an appropriately negative attitude, such as indignation.[19] In this view, the object of the wrongdoer's desert is the attitude itself. Punishment is justified, according to this argument, because the intentional infliction of harm effectively conveys the appropriate anger in a way that a coolly philosophical letter would not.

Part of the appeal of making the negative reactive attitude the object of desert is that it helps block the objection that punishment treats the

---

[16] Feinberg, "The Expressive Function of Punishment," 116.
[17] Ibid.
[18] Another objection is: just because the message is appropriate, it does not follow that I am permitted to deliver that message. This raises the issue of the authority to punish, which I take up in Chapter 3.
[19] Christopher Bennett, *The Apology Ritual: A Philosophical Theory of Punishment* (New York: Cambridge University Press, 2008); and Zac Cogley, "Basic Desert of Reactive Emotions," *Philosophical Explorations* 16, no. 2 (2013): 165–77.

wrongdoer as a mere means, who can simply be used for the benefit of others. Attitudes of resentment and indignation themselves include a kind of recognition of the wrongdoer's status. One does not resent or become indignant with an animal or an object. These are attitudes that can be directed intelligibly only toward a fellow moral agent, someone who stands in relations of mutual accountability with oneself. So to hold a reactive attitude toward a wrongdoer is itself a way of showing him respect. As P. F. Strawson puts it, resenting someone is "the consequence of *continuing* to view him as a member of the moral community; only as one who has offended against its demands."[20] Indeed, failures to adopt an attitude of resentment or indignation toward a wrongdoer, at least initially, are worrying. They suggest that one views the wrongdoer as if he were a child or an animal – as if he were not a fully competent member of the moral community.

The reactive attitude account also seems to avoid the charge of blood-thirstiness. Being targeted with an attitude like resentment or indignation is unpleasant. But these are significantly different attitudes from malice or spite, which aim at the degradation of their target.[21] Resentment and indignation engage the wrongdoer as a rational moral agent, communicating an appropriate attitude to the wrongdoer that hopefully will inspire him to take the proper view of his past actions. If he does take a proper view, he will feel remorse, and remorse is painful. But while this pain may be the inevitable side effect of the successful communication of the attitude, we need not view it as the intrinsic good sought by punishment.

In my opinion, this is a compelling defense of rebuke. Rebukes are direct, angry communications of blame. The harms that they intentionally inflict are limited to the harms that are inseparable from the communication of the intrinsically appropriate attitudes. Since I have argued that rebukes are typically punishments, it is a pretty good justification of at least this method of punishment. But notice how limited this victory is. The account defends private rebukes but not public rebukes. After all, public rebukes intentionally impose further harms, such as damage to reputation and the exposure of the wrongdoer to the shaming gaze of an audience. These go beyond the harm that is inseparable from the communication of moral anger to the wrongdoer. The argument also falls short of defending

[20] P. F. Strawson, "Freedom and Resentment," *Proceedings of the British Academy* 48 (1962): 187–211, at 207. See also Stephen Darwall, "Justice and Retaliation," *Philosophical Papers* 39, no. 3 (2010): 315–41.
[21] Jeffrie G. Murphy and Jean Hampton, *Forgiveness and Mercy* (New York: Cambridge University Press, 1988), 60–79.

practices of pointed social avoidance, which purposefully withdraws the benefits of cooperation and social contact, and boycotting, which directly targets reputation and revenue.

Interestingly, R. A. Duff, who is a leading proponent of censure theories of punishment, rejects the reactive attitude account even for the limited case of private rebuke.[22] Duff dislikes the suggestion that the object of desert is resentment or indignation. In his view, intentionally penalizing someone with one's moral anger is a way of playing on his self-esteem, his desire for good will, and his unconscious fears of abandonment. Emotionally attacking a person in this way in order to get him to change his moral views or his behavior amounts to an objectionable form of manipulation, according to Duff. The one punished is treated as a mere means rather than an end in himself.

Duff explains the sense in which targeting a wrongdoer with negative attitudes is objectionably manipulative by claiming that it offers the wrongdoer the wrong kind of reason for changing his behavior.[23] The wrongdoer is induced to improve his behavior in order to avoid unpleasant consequences. At best, he is offered a prudential reason to behave morally. At worst, the threats and penalties sidestep the wrongdoer's rational capabilities altogether and amount to a kind of "conditioning or aversion therapy."[24]

3.4 Object of Desert: Persuasion

Duff does not disapprove of delivering rebukes or punishment more generally. What he objects to is the suggestion that what the wrongdoer deserves is to be targeted with angry emotions. The proper view of censure, according to Duff, is that it presents the wrongdoer with a *moral* reason to change his behavior.[25] Duff gives us the example of Jasper, who has been sexually harassing women in his office, intimidating and humiliating them through his sexual comments and leers. Suppose we, Jasper's coworkers, witness this behavior. We want Jasper to stop his harassment. We want to protect the women in the office from harm and insult. Duff argues that in order to treat Jasper as a rational moral agent, and not merely as a nuisance, our goal must be that he changes his behavior for the right reason.

---

[22] R. A. Duff, *Trials and Punishments* (New York: Cambridge University Press, 1991), ch. 2.
[23] Ibid., 45–46.
[24] Ibid., 46.
[25] Ibid., 47.

We want him to treat these women decently because he comes to see that they deserve respect, not merely because he wants to keep his job or because he is intimidated by our anger.

When we censure Jasper, according to Duff, we are engaging him in a kind of moral argument or dialogue.[26] We are attempting to persuade him to change his behavior by pointing to the real reasons for change – the reasons we sincerely believe are the proper reasons for treating his coworkers differently. Perhaps Jasper has not so far perceived his behavior as an instance of bullying or oppression. We hope that, in signaling our moral disapproval, we are directing Jasper's attention to values that he already shares. If he does not already share those values, then we hope that by voicing our own commitment to those values, we will persuade him to reevaluate the issues. But Duff argues that respectful censuring, like persuasion more generally, also requires us to be open to Jasper's side of the argument. We must be prepared to listen to his excuses or justifications for his behavior with a kind of humility that acknowledges that our own moral judgments are fallible.[27]

Duff's account of moral censure as a form of persuasion is certainly appealing. It portrays censure as a very high-minded sort of activity, animated by concern for the well-being of the wrongdoer. Yet, intuitively, there is a big difference between engaging in persuasion, as we normally think of persuasion, and punishments like rebuking a wrongdoer or boycotting a business.[28] Persuasion can take place via a dispassionate exchange of ideas and reasons. Rebukes express anger. Boycotts target reputations and revenue. Persuasion tries to attract the other person to one's side. Punishments issue a demand. They draw a line. They press a claim. Persuasion implies that the other person is free to disagree, though disagreement would be mistaken and maybe even imprudent. Punishments insist that the other person has done what he was not free to do *and enforce that judgment.*

Communicative theorists generally argue that sometimes only punishment, only the intentional infliction of harm, can communicate the seriousness of the moral matters at issue.[29] Words are often not strong enough. But punishing actions, like consumer boycotts, can both convey

[26] Ibid. See also Duff, *Punishment, Communication, and Community.*
[27] Duff, *Trials and Punishments,* 52.
[28] Cf. Brenda M. Baker, "Penance as a Model for Punishment," *Social Theory and Practice* 18, no. 3 (1992): 311–32.
[29] Duff, *Punishment, Communication, and Community,* 107. See also Hampton, "Correcting Harms versus Righting Wrongs," and Bennett, *The Apology Ritual.*

the depth of our moral concerns and hold the wrongdoers' attention for long enough to inspire change. But still, Duff interprets these punishments as forms of persuasion.

I agree with Duff and other communicative theorists that the harsher aspects of punishment perform communicative functions, but I believe we must acknowledge the fact that they also operate in other, less high-minded, more manipulative ways as well. While we may intend our rebukes and boycotts to serve as a respectful attempt to persuade a fellow member of the Kingdom of Ends of the error of his ways, our punishments may instead have their effect on the wrongdoer by playing on his vulnerabilities. We may hope to lead the wrongdoer to recognize the validity of our claim. But we may instead merely intimidate and manipulate him. Furthermore, we are, or should be, aware of both of these aspects of the interaction when we engage in punishment.

3.5 Another Option: Limit the Role of Desert

I have argued that appealing to the communication of deserved moral judgments and attitudes is not sufficient to justify the intentional infliction of harm on a wrongdoer. Recently, T. M. Scanlon has presented a version of a communicative theory that suggests that we need not even try to do so.[30] Scanlon argues that there are two elements in punishment: a message of condemnation and hard treatment. The wrongdoer intrinsically deserves condemnation, and this negative desert is sufficient to justify the condemnatory aspect of punishment. But in Scanlon's theory it does not also justify the hard treatment of punishment. In particular, Scanlon declines to argue that hard treatment is justified as an expression of deserved condemnation, since a response to wrongdoing "could express condemnation without involving any form of 'hard treatment.'"[31] We could use Feinberg's rituals of music and drama, for example. Scanlon argues that the hard treatment of punishment must be justified by something other than desert. He appeals to "the beneficial consequences of a policy of threatening and inflicting treatment of this kind" combined with the requirement that the one punished had a "fair opportunity to avoid" wrongdoing.[32] In this way, Scanlon's defense of punishment mixes desert-based and

---

[30] Scanlon, "Giving Desert Its Due."
[31] Ibid., 103.
[32] Ibid., 108.

instrumental considerations, such that desert justifies only the condemnatory aspects of punishment.

Although I also advocate a mixed rather than a purely desert-based strategy for justifying punishment, I do not believe Scanlon's version includes a robust enough desert element. The trouble is that what is deserved (condemnation) and what is received (hard treatment) are not sufficiently closely related. While, in Scanlon's theory, negative desert serves as a side constraint on who receives hard treatment, the hard treatment is not itself deserved nor is it an unavoidable side effect of the treatment that is deserved.

3.6 Object of Desert: Censure Plus Coercive Pressure

The central flaw in all of these variations on expressivist and communicative justifications of punishment is that they concentrate their attention on the high-minded, symbolic aspect of punishment and ignore the ugly, coercive aspect. But punishment has both of these sides, and if we are going to find a justification for punishment we cannot deny the reality of the ugly side. When communicative theorists argue that Feinberg's imagined rituals of music and drama would not have the ability to communicate condemnation in a sufficiently powerful way and that only punishment will do, I suspect they are sweeping coercion under the rug of symbolism. They mean, I think, that music and drama will not keep wrongdoers in line. They are not really concerned about communicative power. They are concerned about coercive power.

I agree with Duff, Scanlon, and others that wrongdoers deserve condemnation. They deserve the negative judgments and attitudes that punishment communicates. However, I do not think that this is a sufficient account of the desert element in punishment. We need to add something more if punishment is to be justifiable.

So let's look at the ugly side of informal social punishments like rebukes and boycotts. There are two things I find important. First, these punishments inflict emotional pressure on the one punished. They play on the wrongdoer's social nature – on her need for human contact and cooperation, on her desire for goodwill from her fellow creatures, on the social underpinnings of her self-esteem, and on her propensity to mirror other people's disapprobation in her own psyche.[33] Second, punishments change the value of the wrongdoer's choice options. Joe's Coffee may continue to

[33] The psychological effects of other people's disapprobation are powerfully described by David Hume, *A Treatise of Human Nature* (New York: Oxford University Press, 2000), and Adam Smith, *Theory of Moral Sentiments* (New York: Penguin, 2010).

treat its employees unfairly, but the boycotters have increased the costs of their doing so. A brother's rebuke may not prevent his sister from lying in the future, or compel her to apologize in the present, but it increases the costs of her poor choices.

By attending to these two features of informal social punishment – the application of emotional pressure and the manipulation of the wrongdoer's options – the coercive aspects of punishment come to the fore. Now, arguably, coercion is only coercion when it is intentional.[34] Our communicative theorist might insist that a morally virtuous punisher will intend only persuasion and not coercion. But I find such a response disingenuous. Punishment places emotional and practical forms of pressure on the one punished, *and* we know this, *and* this is at least part of why we choose to punish rather than merely to criticize. The knowing and purposeful application of pressure to the wrongdoer separates a punishment like the boycott of Joe's Coffee from a merely natural penalty, such as the simple choice to buy one's coffee from a more congenial provider.

Punishment – not just criminal punishment but also social punishment – is a form of coercion. If punishing is justifiable, then coercion must be justifiable. If we are to avoid making the one being controlled a mere means for the betterment of other people, then we must argue that coercion can be deserved. How might we do this? Well, one option is simply to argue that wrongdoers intrinsically deserve to be interfered with. The limitation of liberty is itself the object of negative desert. Wrongdoers intrinsically deserve to have less liberty, less freedom from manipulation, than people who are not guilty of wrongdoing.

In support of this claim, we might cite the view, advocated by Mill and more recently by Stephen Darwall, that moral obligations just are those

---

[34] I have in mind Robert Nozick's account of coercion, helpfully summarized here by Scott Anderson:
"*P* coerces *Q* if and only if:
1. *P* aims to keep *Q* from choosing to perform action *A*;
2. *P* communicates a claim to *Q*;
3. *P*'s claim indicates that if *Q* performs *A*, then *P* will bring about some consequence that would make *Q*'s *A*-ing less desirable to *Q* than *Q*'s not *A*-ing;
4. *P*'s claim is credible to *Q*;
5. *Q* does not do A;
6. Part of *Q*'s reason for not doing *A* is to lessen the likelihood that *P* will bring about the consequence announced in (3)."
Scott Anderson, "Coercion," in *Stanford Encyclopedia of Philosophy*, ed. Edward N. Zalta (2011), plato.stanford.edu. However, I prefer dropping conditions (5) and (6), which imply that an act counts as coercion only if it succeeds in changing the target's behavior. See also Joel Feinberg, *Harm to Self: The Moral Limits of the Criminal Law*, vol. 3 (New York: Oxford University Press, 1989), ch. 23.

things that people can demand from one another.[35] For Mill, to say one is subject to a demand is to say that one is subject to some degree of coercion if one fails to satisfy that demand:

> It is a part of the notion of Duty in every one of its forms, that a person may rightfully be compelled to fulfil it. Duty is a thing which may be *exacted* from a person.... Unless we think that it might be exacted from him, we do not call it his duty.... I think there is no doubt that this distinction lies at the bottom of the notions of right and wrong; that we call any conduct wrong, or employ, instead, some other term of dislike or disparagement, according as we think that the person ought, or ought not, to be punished for it; and we say that it would be right to do so and so, or merely that it would be desirable or laudable, according as we would wish to see the person whom it concerns, compelled, or only persuaded and exhorted, to act in that manner.[36]

In this passage, Mill is making a conceptual connection between wrongdoing and liability to coercion. Whereas Mill ultimately defends the worldview that connects these two concepts on utilitarian grounds, it is open to us to instead interpret the connection in terms of desert. Wrongdoing deserves to be met with a loss of liberty. Wrongdoing deserves coercive interference.

In Chapter 1, I argued that we should not, *as a matter of definition*, insist that the harms required for punishment compromise what would have otherwise been a right. However, according to the view I am defending here – that the object of desert in cases of wrongdoing is a limitation of liberty – the harm does appear to touch on a right. Arguably, people generally have a moral right not to be subjected to the intentional manipulation of their emotions and their choice options, even when the manipulation in question is carried out simply through speech or social avoidance. On this interpretation, informal social punishment does involve treating people in ways that they would normally have a moral right not to be treated.

If this is correct, we might supplement this view of desert with a rights-forfeiture defense of punishment.[37] The idea here is that

---

[35] John Stuart Mill, *Utilitarianism*, in *Collected Works of John Stuart Mill*, vol. 10, ed. J. M. Robson (Toronto: University of Toronto Press, 1969), ch. V; and Stephen Darwall, *The Second-Person Standpoint: Morality, Respect and Accountability* (Cambridge, MA: Harvard University Press, 2006), 14.

[36] Mill, *Utilitarianism*, V.14.

[37] Christopher Heath Wellman, "The Rights Forfeiture Theory of Punishment," *Ethics* 122, no. 2 (2012): 371–93; and A. John Simmons, "Locke and the Right to Punish," *Philosophy and Public Affairs* 20 (1991): 311–49.

the wrongdoer forfeits some portion of her rights through her own, responsible choice to act wrongly. Forfeiture theorists have traditionally suggested that what the wrongdoer forfeits is her right not to be subjected to suffering. This suggestion is open to the charge of blood-thirstiness. It suggests that the rest of us are eager to inflict suffering on whomever loses the protection of the right, as if we cannot wait to let out our aggression somewhere. My suggestion is instead that the thing forfeited is some measure of liberty, some right against being intentionally coerced by other people.

My version of forfeiture theory is less disturbing than the one that focuses on suffering, but one might still object that the view implies that the power to control other people is an intrinsically desirable good. Are we eager to manipulate people as soon as they lose the protection of the right? Are we thirsty, not for blood, but for domination?

I want to acknowledge the legitimacy of this worry. As Nietzsche said, we should be suspicious of people in whom the urge to punish is strong.[38] However, I hope that we can distinguish between justified punishment and this sort of thirst for domination. While the view I am defending here suggests that wrongdoers forfeit their right against being subjected to coercion, I am not saying that they may be subjected to coercion *in any direction whatsoever*. What the wrongdoer deserves is not manipulation *simply as such*, but only manipulation toward certain ends. To fill out this account, we must turn to the instrumental half of this mixed theory of punishment.

This brings to a close my long and winding discussion of the object of desert in cases of wrongdoing. I argue that what wrongdoing intrinsically deserves is both the communication of censure and coercive pressure. In the end, I both agree and disagree with communicative theorists like Duff. I agree that communication is an important part of a theory of punishment. But communicative theorists interpret punishment simply as moral messages to the wrongdoer. My point is that punishments are also forms of coercion. In other words, whereas a communicative theorist interprets social control as moral communication, I see certain kinds of moral communication, like angry rebukes and boycotts, as social control.

---

[38] Friedrich Nietzsche, *Thus Spake Zarathustra*, trans. Thomas Wayne (New York: Algora, 2003).

4 THE INSTRUMENTAL ELEMENT IN A CONSTRAINED
INSTRUMENTALIST APPROACH

Joel Feinberg points out that the fact that someone deserves something is not necessarily a conclusive reason for giving him what he deserves.[39] My view is that negative desert justifies interfering with the liberty of wrongdoers only if doing so will also achieve some future good. Let's turn now to the forward-looking aspects of informal social punishment. What kinds of good consequences might informal social punishment achieve?

The first thing that comes to mind is deterrence. One possible good effect of practices like rebuking and boycotting is that they may deter future wrongdoing, either by the one punished or by others who wish to avoid punishment.

We might argue further that informal social punishment is instrumental to the maintenance of moral norms.[40] Unless moral norms are enforced, unless our moral demands of one another are backed up with some form of social pressure, they will cease to effectively regulate social life. So, one reason to engage in informal social punishment in response to moral wrongdoing is to maintain those norms.

Punishing wrongdoers is also a means of vindicating the victims of wrongdoing.[41] By boycotting Joe's Coffee, customers send the message to the workers that they are valuable persons who deserve better treatment. This may reinforce the workers' self-worth and help undermine the power of the insulting messages conveyed by their employer's unjust actions. When one is oneself the victim, rebuking the wrongdoer can be a means of both defending oneself and shoring up one's self-respect.

In some cases, punishing wrongdoers enables third parties to avoid complicity in the wrongdoing in question. Such arguments are frequently made in support of boycotting actions. The idea is that the consumer must avoid contributing to the market dynamics that enable business owners to profit from their misdeeds. Similarly, standing passively by as another person is mistreated may itself be a way of insulting or morally abandoning

---

[39] Joel Feinberg, "Justice and Personal Desert," in *Doing and Deserving: Essays in the Theory of Responsibility* (Princeton: Princeton University Press, 1970), 55–94, at 60.
[40] William A. Edmundson, "Civility as Political Constraint," *Res Publica* 8, no. 3 (2002): 217–29; and J. R. Lucas, "Or Else," *Proceedings of the Aristotelian Society* 69 (1968): 207–22, at 214.
[41] Cf. Hampton, "Correcting Harms versus Righting Wrongs"; Bennett, *The Apology Ritual*.

the victim.[42] For example, studies of bullying indicate that the presence of passive bystanders increases the psychological and social harms suffered by the bullied children.[43]

So, informal social punishment might provide benefits to both communities and victims. But one might object that there is still something offensive in using the wrongdoer as a mere means to securing these benefits to others. At this point, theorists pursuing a mixed strategy to defending punishment standardly appeal to the desert element. It is not objectionable to punish one person as a means to benefiting others as long as the one punished is guilty. The guilty one has lost some measure of her right not to be interfered with, so interfering in ways that will benefit others is not objectionable.

In my view, this line of defense is not quite satisfying. Yes, the wrongdoer has forfeited a measure of her liberty; she deserves to be interfered with; but she is still a moral agent with legitimate interests and dignity. For these reasons, I argue that any interference with the wrongdoer should be designed with an eye to the wrongdoer's good, as well as the good of the victim and the community. More specifically, we should design our interference so as to support her abilities as a moral agent and to help her reclaim her place as a trusted member of the moral community. In doing so, we apply coercion to the wrongdoer with the goal of bringing about a state of affairs in which coercive interference with her would no longer be fitting. When the punisher's coercive interference aims at its own cessation in this way, hopefully the punisher's temptation to the vicious pleasures of dominating another person will be kept in check.

5 THE MORAL PRESSURE THEORY OF PUNISHMENT

I suggest that the proper goal of informally socially punishing a wrongdoer – the aim we should have when interfering with her liberty – is to morally pressure her to make amends for her own misdeed. The pressure is moral in the sense that it promotes a moral goal – the wrongdoer fulfilling her obligation to make amends or "atone" – and it communicates moral reasons for fulfilling that goal. But it is a form of pressure as well as a form

[42] Jean Harvey, "Oppression, Moral Abandonment, and the Role of Protest," *Journal of Social Philosophy* 27, no. 1 (1996): 156–71; and Margaret Urban Walker, *Moral Repair: Reconstructing Moral Relations after Wrongdoing* (New York: Cambridge University Press, 2006).
[43] Paul D. Flaspohler, Jennifer L. Elfstrom, Karin L. Vanderzee, Holli E. Sink, and Zachary Birchmeier, "Stand by Me: The Effects of Peer and Teacher Support in Mitigating the Impact of Bullying on Quality of Life," *Psychology in the Schools* 46, no. 7 (2009): 636–49.

of communication. If we have a proper view of the obligation to atone, then we will see that atonement serves the interests of the victim, community, and the wrongdoer herself.[44]

In order to make amends, the wrongdoer must, by her own actions and to whatever degree it is possible, repair whatever wrongs she has committed and harms she has caused, including the harms she has done to her relationships of mutual respect and goodwill with other people. What the obligation to atone requires in practice will vary from case to case, depending on the nature and severity of the wrongs and harms, the relationship between the wrongdoer and the victim, and the capabilities of the wrongdoer. But the making of amends typically requires three things from the wrongdoer: moral improvement, respectful communication, and the reparation of harm.

First, moral improvement requires ceasing the wrongful action and committing oneself not to repeat it. The owners and managers of Joe's Coffee, in our example, must change their abusive scheduling practices. But they should also recognize that their practices were *unjust*, not merely bad for business. A natural consequence of recognizing their responsibility for wrongdoing will be a feeling of guilt and remorse, but such painful feelings are not themselves to be counted as intrinsic goods in a theory of atonement but as side effects of moral improvement in the aftermath of wrongdoing.[45] The second part of the obligation to atone requires the wrongdoers to communicate respectfully with the victims. The owners and managers of Joe's Coffee should apologize to their employees and assure them that they now recognize their legitimate interests. The third part of the obligation to atone is to repair the harms created wherever possible. For Joe's Coffee, this might involve paying compensation for unfairly reduced hours or rehiring workers who quit or were fired as a result of unreasonable scheduling practices.

Atonement benefits victims, providing them with apologies, reparations, and some assurance against future victimization. Atonement benefits communities by deterring wrongdoing and clarifying norms. But atonement also benefits the wrongdoer. By making proper amends, the owners and managers of Joe's Coffee would improve themselves and reestablish their relationships of mutual respect, goodwill, and trust with their employees and customers.

---

[44] I defend the following account of the nature of making amends in Linda Radzik, *Making Amends: Atonement in Morality, Law, and Politics* (New York: Oxford University Press, 2009).
[45] Ibid., 86–90.

In earlier work, I presented something like this as an "atonement theory of punishment."[46] But this puts the emphasis in the wrong place. Only wrongdoers atone. The ones punishing cannot atone for them, since atonement requires sincere changes in beliefs and attitudes and not just in behavior.[47] All punishers can do is to motivate atonement through communication and the application of emotional and practical forms of pressure. The justifiability of punishment turns on what the punishers do.

If the communicative aspects of punishment are well designed, they will tell the wrongdoer that his action was wrong. They will draw the wrongdoer's attention to the costs of his transgression, including negative reactive attitudes, and the weakening of trust and goodwill among his fellows. Such costs are likely even in the absence of a decision to punish; they include what I have been calling the natural penalties of wrongdoing. But a well-designed punishment will also tell the wrongdoer that there is something that he can do to put things right. If the coercive aspects of punishment are well designed, they create incentives for the wrongdoer to reform his attitudes and behaviors, apologize, and pay reparations; and they do so without undermining the moral capacities and motivations the wrongdoer needs in order to atone properly.[48]

In cases of informal social punishment, the means of coercion that punishers are legally and morally permitted to use are unlikely to be strong enough to compel wrongdoers to change their behaviors or pay reparations. At least in ordinary contexts, the state will have a

---

[46] Radzik, "Moral Rebukes and Social Avoidance."

[47] The importance of sincerity is a point on which I disagree with Duff's "penance" account of punishment and especially his view of apology (Duff, *Punishment, Communication, and Community*, 106ff.). Also, Duff seems to suggest that the experience of suffering itself, and particularly the suffering of remorse, helps satisfy the wrongdoer's obligation to atone. In my view, the suffering of remorse is only a side effect or symptom of the changes in attitudes that are required for atonement (Radzik, *Making Amends*, 86–90).

[48] The moral pressure theory bears some resemblance to a moral education theory of punishment. According to that sort of approach, the proper goal of punishment is the moral improvement of the wrongdoer. See, for example, Jean Hampton, "The Moral Education Theory of Punishment," *Philosophy and Public Affairs* 13, no. 3 (1984): 208–38. However, Hampton, who was at one time a leading proponent of this theory, came to reject it because she felt that it did not give proper recognition to the victims of wrongdoing (Murphy and Hampton, *Forgiveness and Mercy*, 130). Punishing a bully merely in order to improve the bully has benefits for her victim, if it works. But Hampton argues that it does not send the sort of message of respect for the victim and caring about his plight that morality requires. It does not put the harms to the victim in a central enough place. In contrast, in pressuring the wrongdoer to make amends, punishment pressures the wrongdoer to respond appropriately *to the victim*. In this way, third parties who engage in informal social punishment show their own respect and caring for the victim.

functioning monopoly on violence. Ordinary individuals interacting with their social equals may not use physical force. But they can and do use coercion. As Mill reminds us, while informal social penalties do not attack the body, they attack the soul.[49] They play on people's emotions and deep-seated psychological and social needs. Yet the coercive power of other people's angry words or social avoidance depends on how much I value their good opinion, company, and cooperation and how willing I am to exit that community and find another community to satisfy my psychological and social needs. In these ways, I can undermine other people's attempts to enforce a system of norms against me through social punishment.[50]

The virtuous punisher should hope that the communicative aspects of punishment will predominate over the coercive aspects. She should prefer that the one punished will make amends for the correct, moral reasons rather than the less worthy, prudential reasons that punishment also provides. Duff argues that prudential reasons are the wrong kinds of reasons for the wrongdoer to change his ways, and that to intentionally create prudential incentives for such changes is to treat him like a dog – like an animal to be trained rather than a person to be reasoned with.[51] But I disagree with Duff that offering the wrongdoer prudential reasons to change his ways is objectionably disrespectful to the wrongdoer.[52] Maintaining social cooperation, cultivating a good reputation in the community, and preserving the goodwill of one's fellows are perfectly legitimate (though not always decisive) reasons for action.[53] Such concerns are prudential but they are not morally insignificant. Joe's Coffee's interest in profit is more purely prudential, but it is already a factor in its relationship with its customers, so it is hard to see the customer's intentional withholding of revenue as a case of treating Joe's

[49] John Stuart Mill, *On Liberty*, in *Collected Works of John Stuart Mill*, vol. 18, ed. J. M. Robson (Toronto: University of Toronto Press, 1977), I.5.
[50] This phenomenon is well illustrated by the use of boycotts on either side of the same-sex marriage debate in the United States prior to its legalization in 2015. Both sides called for boycotts against businesses that supported what they considered to be the wrong side of the debate. The boycotted businesses often found themselves receiving an influx of new customers or donations from people who sympathized with their position. In some cases, business owners seemed to take pride in being boycotted by people whose politics they despised.
[51] Duff, *Punishment, Communication, and Community*, 85.
[52] Cf. Baker, "Penance as a Model of Punishment"; von Hirsch, *Censure and Sanctions*; and Matt Matravers, "Duff on Hard Treatment," in *Crime, Punishment and Responsibility*, ed. R. Cruft, M. Kramer and M. Reiff (New York: Oxford University Press, 2011), 68–86.
[53] Claudia Mills, "Should We Boycott Boycotts?," *Journal of Social Philosophy* 27, no. 3 (1996): 136–48, at 140.

Coffee with disrespect.[54] The coercive aspects of punishment do not necessarily deny respect to the one punished.

6 CONCLUSION

In this chapter, I have argued that the general justifying aim of informal social punishment is to morally pressure the wrongdoer to atone. Part of the value of identifying an account of the justifying aim of punishment is that it can help yield a set of restrictions on actual practices and acts of punishment. For example, if I am correct in identifying the moral pressure to atone as the aim of informal social punishment, then it will follow that punishing acts that undermine wrongdoer's ability to atone, or that pile on wrongdoers who have already atoned, will be unjustified. Such limitations on punishment will be the focus of Chapter 3.

In this chapter, I have followed a mixed strategy, a version of constrained instrumentalism, which uses a claim about the wrongdoer's desert to constrain the ways in which punishment can be used to pursue good future outcomes. In acting wrongly, one comes to deserve both censure and a loss of liberty. Only wrongdoers may be subjected to informal social punishment, but negative desert is not a sufficient justification for punishment. A wrongdoer may be subjected to coercion only insofar as such an action has a reasonable chance of motivating the wrongdoer to atone. In Chapter 3, I inquire into what sorts of methods and practices tend to support or else undermine the proper aims of punishment. I also – finally – take on the question of who has the authority to impose informal social punishment for what sorts of moral wrongs. What I have tried to do here is address a quite general question: the question of what – if anything – could count as a legitimate reason for engaging in informal social punishment. I believe that the answer that I have provided makes it plausible that punishments like rebukes and boycotts are at least potentially permissible and even valuable in practice.

But let me also emphasize what I have *not* tried to do here. I have not offered a justification of punishment in general. I have not recommended the moral pressure to atone as the goal of *criminal punishment*. Law and morality are not coextensive. The liberal state is properly neutral among reasonable conceptions of the good, and properly restricts its use of force to

---

[54] Things can get complicated, of course. Were Joe's customers to manipulate the profit motive in order to get the owners and managers to do something against their sincere and reasonable moral consciences, then the boycotters may not be treating them with respect.

control its citizens' behaviors rather than their consciences. The prospect of the state using its monopoly on violence to press for atonement is in part so frightening because it does not allow alleged wrongdoers sufficient opportunity to opt out of the system of values being enforced. In contrast, informal social penalties generally leave their targets with more latitude for resistance.

Note further that I have not presented the moral pressure account as the general justifying aim of *formal* social punishment. Here, the complication is that there are so many different kinds of hierarchically structured institutions that practice formal social punishment, including families, clubs, schools, religious and political organizations, and businesses. Perhaps some of these punishers – like parents or religious leaders – would be justified in using coercion to motivate wrongdoers to fulfill their moral obligation to atone, but others, like employers, arguably lack the authority to do so. Like the state, employers might intrude too far into people's lives and consciences by pressing them improve. On the other hand, this could well depend on the nature of the employment, such that members of professions or employees who present the public face of the organization might legitimately be held to a higher standard.

Social institutions vary so widely that I am tempted to put the topic of formal social punishment to one side altogether. But Chapter 3 will show just how hard it is to do this. As we dig into the details of practicing informal social punishment, my examples will highlight the phenomenon of naming and shaming in social media. Ordinary people witness someone committing a wrong and publicly call the wrongdoer out on the social media. If you have paid any attention to cases like these, you know what typically comes next: the wrongdoer gets fired.

CHAPTER 3

Practicing Social Punishment

Linda Radzik

I INTRODUCTION

In Chapter 2, I argued that the proper goal of informal social punishment for moral wrongdoing is to pressure culpable actors to make amends. I called this the "moral pressure" theory of punishment and suggested that, when this goal of pressuring wrongdoers to make amends is kept in mind, punishment can reinforce moral norms, support victims, and deter wrongdoing while at the same time helping the wrongdoers to do what they should be doing anyway and showing them a robust form of respect. In this third chapter, I argue that, even when one has the correct aim, a multitude of factors may still render informal social punishment unjust or unwise. Punishment might be applied for the right reason but by the wrong person, using the wrong method, to the wrong degree, at the wrong moment, or against the wrong target. The ethical practice of social punishment requires great sensitivity to context, including things such as the relationship between the punisher and the punished, the nature and severity of the wrong committed, and the legitimate interests of any particular victims and communities. Here, I provide an overview of these complexities by examining the phenomenon of naming and shaming on the Internet. I then defend a handful of restrictions on informal social punishment.[1]

The first set of restrictions emerges when we think more carefully about what it means for a wrongdoer to atone and for a punisher to help motivate that atonement. These reflections yield some general, though defeasible, reasons for preferring certain methods of punishing over others. Second, I argue that, frequently, only some people will have the authority to punish a

---

[1] Brief passages below appear in Linda Radzik, "Moral Rebukes and Social Avoidance," *Journal of Value Inquiry* 48, no. 4 (2014): 643–61; and "Bystanders and Shared Responsibility," in *Routledge Handbook of Collective Responsibility*, ed. Deborah Tollefsen and Saba Bazargan-Forward (New York: Routledge, 2020).

particular wrong. I sketch two different approaches to developing a theory of authority that would support this conclusion, and explain why I prefer one of them. My goal is to argue for ethical principles that can help rein in overactive practices of informal social punishment. At the end of the chapter, I consider the view that our standards for social punishment should be more permissive in cases involving systematic oppression, such as those targeted by the #MeToo and #LivingWhileBlack online movements.

2 NAMING AND SHAMING IN SOCIAL MEDIA

In order to spur our thinking about just how messy and morally fraught informal social punishment can become, there is no better place to look than online. Social media has turned out to be a powerful tool for the infliction of informal social punishment. The most popular method is naming and shaming. It typically goes something like this: someone does something that someone else (perhaps a victim, perhaps not) perceives as morally objectionable. This witness then communicates that the act was wrong and the actor was culpable to an audience that includes other parties as well as the wrongdoer.[2]

In some cases, the other audience members were previously unaware of the objectionable action. Many posts using the #MeToo hashtag fit this pattern. Someone publicly reports that a particular person harassed or assaulted her on a particular occasion. A twist on this kind of shaming by reporting involves victims or witnesses filming the wrongful incident in progress on their smartphones and then posting the videos. Readers are likely familiar with the cases of bystanders filming police misconduct. But people are also filming noncriminal wrongdoing, such as people behaving rudely in public, as in the case of Dog Poop Girl in South Korea from 2005.[3] A young woman refused to clean up after her dog on the subway. Someone filmed her and posted the video. It went viral, and soon the woman's name and address were also posted online.

---

[2] Often, the inclusion of the wrongdoer is indirect. I can name and shame my coworker with a tweet even if she is not on Twitter, as long as it is predictable that she will come to hear about it. Condemnations that are intentionally designed to take place behind the wrongdoer's back are cases of gossip rather than naming and shaming. See Linda Radzik, "Gossip and Social Punishment," *Res Philosophica* 93, no. 1, (2016): 185–204.

[3] Hanne Detel, "Disclosure and Public Shaming in the Age of New Visibility," in *Media and Public Shaming: Drawing the Boundaries of Disclosure*, ed. Julian Petley (New York: I. B. Tauris, 2013), 77–96; and Mark Tunick, *Balancing Privacy and Free Speech: Unwanted Attention in the Age of Social Media* (New York: Routledge, 2015), ch. 1.

In other cases of naming and shaming, the namer addresses an audience that already knows about the action in question, but may not perceive it as wrong. Here the witness is not reporting what was done but instead testifying that the act was wrong. For example, one person posts a comment to his "friends" on Facebook that trades in demeaning stereotypes of a racial group. One of those friends sends a reply labeling the original comment as racist, and this reply is visible to the audience that received the original post. Online communities where this second type of naming and shaming are common are sometimes described as participating in "call-out culture."[4] The label suggests a particularly high readiness among community members to police interactions and publicly identify transgressions and transgressors.

A recent variation on naming and shaming involves declaring that the wrongdoer is "canceled." Such declarations seem to operate as both public shaming and calls for social withdrawal from the condemned person. A prominent example involves the singer R. Kelly, who has been accused of repeated instances of sexual, physical, and emotional abuse.[5] The hashtag #MuteRKelly was used to encourage people not only to refrain from buying new music and merchandise from Kelly but also to discard any products they already own and to appeal to others not to play his music publicly. By declaring a wrongdoer canceled, one resolves, and encourages others to resolve, to deny the wrongdoer a public platform.[6]

Some instances of calling people out online might be better described as moral criticism than as informal social punishment. Following Elise Springer's conception, we can describe moral criticism as a form of communication that draws attention to a matter of moral concern.[7] One can morally criticize without making a definitive moral judgment about

[4] Alyssa Teekah, "Lessons from SlutWalk: How Call-Out Culture Hurts Our Movement," *Herizons* 29, no. 2 (2015): 16–21.

[5] Jacey Fortin, "R. Kelly's Two-Decade Trail of Sexual Abuse Accusations," *New York Times*, online edition, May 10, 2018.

[6] Criticism of "canceling" often suggests that it is a sign that our culture has become less tolerant than it used to be. (See, for example, Emily S. Rueb and Derrick Bryson Taylor, "Obama on Call-Out Culture: 'That's Not Activism,'" *New York Times*, online edition, Oct. 31, 2019.) But canceling resembles some older practices of informal social punishment. Recall how groups of concerned citizens, such as the Moral Majority, used to pressure broadcasters to uphold standards of "decency" for television and radio. There, too, protestors aimed to deny positions of public influence to those who promoted or embodied values of which they disapproved. These days, the protestors in question are more loosely organized and often represent the concerns of marginalized populations rather than traditional, conservative values (Ernest Owens, "Obama's Very Boomer View of 'Cancel Culture,'" *New York Times*, online edition, Nov. 1, 2019).

[7] Elise Springer, *Communicating Moral Concern: An Ethics of Critical Responsiveness* (Cambridge, MA: MIT Press, 2013).

rightness or wrongness or about culpability. Criticism may be simply an invitation to shared moral reflection. Informal social punishment, on the other hand, involves the intentional infliction of a harm that expresses reprobation. Instances of naming and shaming frequently fall into a gray area between moral criticism and informal social punishment. This area is gray indeed. Our motivations are not always transparent to us. The risk of self-deception here is high, since people are frequently unwilling to acknowledge their own aggression and desires to coerce other people. Furthermore, from the point of view of both the person being called out and the audience members in front of whom he is called out, the shaming may be just as great whether the "namer" intends to punish or merely to engage in shared moral reflection.

Naming and shaming are so tightly intertwined that it would be artificial to separate them into different actions. It is the public naming that shames. If I simply post on Twitter, "John did x," knowing that x will be disapproved of by the audience, I do not need to say anything else in order to express my reprobation. I do not have to say, "John is an awful person," and neither does my audience. John is likely to be harmed simply by exposure to the critical gaze of others.[8] Audiences often do not stay silent, though. They pile on, voicing their own condemnations.[9] Things sometimes snowball. More and more people comment on the incident, often one-upping each other with the intensity or the wittiness of their condemnations. Incidents can spread to other formats and even larger audiences.[10] Traditional media sources like newspapers treat widespread outbreaks of indignation on Twitter as newsworthy events and publish stories about them. When things really heat up, it can get very ugly. Hateful speech, violent imagery, rape threats, and death threats are not uncommon online.

Journalist Jon Ronson documented a number of naming and shaming incidents in his 2015 book, *So You've Been Publicly Shamed*.[11] Some of them involve the punishment of public figures for various kinds of trans-gressions. But, as in the case of Dog Poop Girl, one need not be a public figure to receive a huge amount of public attention. Ronson recounts the story of an ordinary, thirty-year-old woman named Justine who posted a

---

[8] Thomas Nagel, "Concealment and Exposure," *Philosophy and Public Affairs* 27, no. 1 (1998): 3–30; and Tunick, *Balancing Privacy and Free Speech*.
[9] Justin Tosi and Brandon Warmke, "Moral Grandstanding," *Philosophy and Public Affairs* 44, no. 3 (2016): 197–217.
[10] Detel, "Disclosure and Public Shaming in the Age of New Visibility."
[11] Jon Ronson, *So You've Been Publicly Shamed* (New York: Riverhead Books, 2015), ch. 4.

joke on Twitter to her 170 followers. Just before boarding a plane from London to Cape Town, she wrote, "Going to Africa. Hope I don't get AIDS. Just kidding. I'm white!" While Justine says she intended the comment to be a critique of racism, it was widely perceived simply as racist. Someone forwarded the tweet to a well-known journalist, who broadcast his condemnation to a much larger audience. It became the top trending topic on Twitter that day. By the time Justine's flight landed in Cape Town, her tweet had received tens of thousands of angry replies. In the end, the total was 100,000 replies. A Twitter user waited for Justine at the Cape Town airport in order to photograph her reaction when she turned her phone on and saw what had become of her tweet. She was quickly fired from her corporate public relations job, and her employer issued a public condemnation. Family members told her she had brought shame on them all. Workers at the hotel where she planned to stay threatened to strike if she was admitted. She was told that "no one could guarantee [her] safety."[12]

Ronson, who interviewed Justine repeatedly over the next year, reports that the psychological and social consequences were severe and likely to be long-lasting. It was difficult for Justine to leave the house, let alone to find new employment. Her sleeplessness, depression, and other symptoms resembled post-traumatic stress disorder. Among her other concerns, Justine wondered how she would ever be able to date again, given that the first thing people of her generation do when meeting a new person is to Google them; and, of course, Google doesn't forget.[13]

Justine's case provides a particularly extreme example of what can happen when informal social punishment meets new media, but it is hardly unique. I suspect most of us can think of examples that have taken place on a smaller scale in our professions, universities, or circles of friends. To my mind, Justine's case provides us with a powerful illustration of John Stuart Mill's claim that social punishment "leaves fewer means of escape [than legal punishment], penetrating much more deeply into the details of life, and enslaving the soul itself."[14] It is for these reasons that Mill warns

---

[12] Ibid., 76.
[13] The European Union has enacted legislation establishing a "right to be forgotten." It provides individuals with legal recourse to having certain information removed or blocked from internet searches, although it is unclear how effective such measures will be. See Jasmine E. McNealy, "The Emerging Conflict between Newsworthiness and the Right to Be Forgotten," *Northern Kentucky Law Review* 39, no. 2 (2012): 119–35.
[14] John Stuart Mill, *On Liberty*, in *Collected Works of John Stuart Mill*, vol. 18, ed. J. M. Robson (Toronto: University of Toronto Press, 1977), I.5. Citations of Mill's works specify chapter and paragraph number.

us that the "moral coercion of public opinion"[15] has the potential to be a form
of "social tyranny more formidable than many kinds of political oppression."[16]
Interestingly, in *On Liberty*, Mill always describes the agent of social punishment as "public opinion" or "society," rather than any particular individual or
group. Perhaps in his day as well as ours, the greatest threat in social
punishment is the threat posed by the mob.

3 OBJECTIONS TO INFORMAL SOCIAL PUNISHMENT

This section catalogs the various ways in which naming and shaming on
social media, and informal social punishment in general, can go wrong.
The first set of problems turns on issues of guilt and innocence. Punishing
acts might be unjust because the action in question is not actually wrong.
This is Ronson's reaction to Justine's case.[17] He believes that her joke was
meant to be a critique of white privilege rather than a gleeful celebration of
it. The joke was just poorly written. Other people might instead judge
Justine's tweet as wrong, but as a milder sort of wrong than the response to
it suggests. One might argue that she is guilty of being crass or obtuse, but
not hateful.

Punishing acts might also go wrong by failing to take account of
circumstances that excuse or mitigate what would otherwise be culpable
actions. For example, perhaps Dog Poop Girl normally does clean up after
her dog, but just ran out of plastic bags or was sick or especially over-
whelmed that day. Notice that the audience for naming and shaming
campaigns, who are in a way both punishers and the instruments of
punishment, often fail to do any independent research at all into the facts
of the case. Justine found it particularly painful that the mob destroyed her
life while knowing only a few things about her.[18] Her critics used a few
sentences written on her Twitter feed to evaluate her entire character.

An important contrast between legal and social punishment is that the
agents of punishment acting on behalf of the state have both the authority
and the resources to collect evidence on questions of guilt. Courts of law
also allow the accused to defend themselves before inflicting punishment.
Twitter does not. The ones punished may be unable to broadcast their
defenses as broadly as their shame was broadcast. Sober corrections of the

[15] Mill, *On Liberty*, I.9.
[16] Ibid., I.5.
[17] Ronson, *So You've Been Publicly Shamed*, 73–74.
[18] Ibid., 74.

record garner far fewer likes and reposts than juicy accusations and witty denunciations. Even if the accused can make themselves heard, the damage may already have been done.

Another contrast between legal and social penalties has to do with disagreement over what counts as wrong. The law sets out a determinate number of crimes, which are formally and publicly defined, and a fairly determinate set of legally allowable defenses. In everyday life, these things are much more contestable. Whether an act is morally wrong, how serious it is, and whether the actor should be excused are all questions that frequently admit of reasonable disagreement.

In addition to problems with guilt determination, injustice can arise from disproportionality between the offense and the punishment. The shaming power of public exposure for wrongdoing does not lend itself to much nuance. We can see this in examples of call-out culture within activist circles. Imagine members of a feminist group who punish political leaders for egregiously sexist behaviors by describing and condemning those behaviors online but then correct fellow activists for using less than fully enlightened turns of phrase by describing and condemning those behaviors online as well. Even if the latter criticisms are expressed in less harsh language or are carefully worded to condemn just the person's action and not the person's character as a whole, we have very similar punishments for wrongs of quite different severity.[19] The punitive power of naming and shaming lies largely in exposing the target to the critical gaze of others, and both the politicians and the fellow activists are so exposed. Ironically, those people who are most alive to the moral concerns in question may be the most vulnerable to the punitive power of naming and shaming. The activists might experience far more harm than the misogynistic politicians.

Problems of disproportionality also arise because the harmfulness of punishment accumulates. A written rebuke to Justine for posting an offensive joke may well have been an appropriately punitive response. But 100,000 written rebukes were surely excessive. Being exposed before a larger audience is generally worse than being exposed to a smaller audience. Condemnations that remain searchable indefinitely on the

---

[19] Similar criticisms have been made of the #MeToo hashtag, which has been used to call out everything from rape and sexual coercion, to offensive language, to moral failures that are harder to pinpoint. For a window on how people are wrestling with the scope of the issues involved, see Avi Selk, "In a Very Dark Sketch, SNL Points Out We Still Don't Know How to Talk about Aziz Ansari," *Washington Post*, online edition, January 28, 2018.

Internet are generally more harmful than private rebukes, which are delivered directly from critic to wrongdoer and away from other witnesses.

Issues of proportionality also arise in legal punishment, of course, but they threaten to be more intractable for informal social punishment. Legal penalties are measured and doled out by a central authority, but public shaming is uncontrollable.[20] The original namer cannot determine how many people will eventually be included in the audience, what their evaluative reactions will be, or what they will do with the information in the future. The original punisher may express his censure in measured and morally nuanced language, yet set off a firestorm of indignation online that includes loss of employment, hate speech, or threats of violence. Once public shaming begins, no one has the power to end it. Apologies from wrongdoers, no matter how well designed, are surprisingly ineffective in these cases.[21] Labor unions and activist groups have learned a similar lesson about consumer boycotts. Boycotts are much easier to begin than to call off.

Another source of problems for naming and shaming and informal social punishment more generally is their vulnerability to ulterior motives. I have argued that the proper intention to bring to informal social punishment is the intention to morally pressure the wrongdoer to make amends. However, that intention may well coexist with, and even help mask, less worthy motives. Social media users enjoy a boost of dopamine when their contributions are liked and reposted.[22] We receive psychological benefits from feeling that we are "in the know" or part of a movement. We like to feel virtuous, to feel *more virtuous* than other people, and to have our virtue witnessed. People sometimes also join in naming and shaming campaigns for fear that silence will signal support for the wrongful action. They join in the shaming for fear of being shamed themselves.

---

[20] Mark Tunick, "Privacy and Punishment," *Social Theory and Practice* 39, no. 4 (2013): 643–68, at 649. One reason why the severity of legal punishment is also hard to control is because it is typically intertwined with social punishment. Being sent to jail is shameful. Employers, neighbors, and potential friends may socially avoid ex-cons. For reasons like these, some European countries protect the identities of criminals. See Jacob Rowbottom, "To Punish, Inform, and Criticise: The Goals of Naming and Shaming," in *Media and Public Shaming: Drawing the Boundaries of Disclosure*, ed. Julian Petley (New York: I. B. Tauris, 2013), 1–18, at 3.

[21] Several attempts at apology are described in Ronson, *So You've Been Publicly Shamed*. Ronson speculates that shamelessness may be a more effective psychic defense against public shaming than atonement (see, e.g., chs. 7, 8, and 13). This is chilling, since the case of the utterly shameless President Trump shows how shamelessness erodes norms.

[22] Jaron Lanier, *Ten Arguments for Deleting Your Social Media Accounts Right Now* (London: Bodley Head, 2018), 8. Lanier's book provides an interesting analysis of social media as an "asshole amplification technology" (44).

Add to this our susceptibility to the pleasures of vengeance and schaden-freude, and the extra temptation when we can indulge our aggressive impulses anonymously. All of these factors help contribute to the snowbal-ling effect in online naming and shaming campaigns like the one that targeted Justine.

Finally, we should acknowledge that informal social punishment can lead to unintended consequences. For example, the consumers who boycott Joe's Coffee in order to protest the mistreatment of workers may wind up doing more harm than good. Joe's Coffee might respond to lower revenues by laying off workers rather than by treating them better. Both boycotting and naming and shaming tend to inspire backlashes. Boycotts of business owners who discriminate against LGBTQ cus-tomers have been met with online campaigns to raise donations for those business owners.[23] The naming and shaming of racism, sexism, and homophobia online are sometimes used as recruiting moments for hate groups.

Another frequent criticism of naming and shaming practices is that they have a chilling effect on speech. When expressing one's views comes with the risk of being publicly vilified, then one may reasonably decide that it is better not to express oneself at all. The result could be a loss of the benefits of discourse all around, including the retreat of individuals into "informa-tion bubbles" where they will interact only with like-minded people who will confirm their opinions.

While there is certainly something to this concern, we have reason to worry that it is raised in biased ways against groups who have traditionally been silenced. As Brittney Cooper argues, members of more privileged groups tend to see their own speech simply as speech (or as objective, reason-based scholarship) even when it insults and harms members of less privileged groups. But when members of the less privileged groups object, their responses tend to be categorized not as counter-speech but as forms of aggression that violate the freedom of the first, privileged speaker.[24] Cooper also reminds us that a right to speak should not be mistaken for the absence of moral accountability for what one chooses to say. The question at issue in this book is what forms that sort of accountability may take.

---

[23] James Queally, "$828,000 Raised for Indiana Pizzeria That Said It Won't Cater Gay Weddings," *Los Angeles Times*, online edition, April 3, 2015.
[24] Brittney Cooper, "How Free Speech Works for White Academics," *Chronicle of Higher Education* 64, no. 13 (2017): 8.

4 RESTRICTIONS ON INFORMAL SOCIAL PUNISHMENT DRAWN FROM THE GENERAL JUSTIFYING AIM

Given all of the ways in which informal social punishment can be unjust or counterproductive, we need ethical principles to help restrain punishment practices. Next I would like to argue that the account of the general justifying aim of punishment, which was developed in Chapter 2, provides some help here.

Recall that the moral pressure account is a version of a mixed theory, or constrained instrumentalism. The proper aim of punishment has both a desert condition and an instrumental condition, such that desert constrains our pursuit of good outcomes. Let's start with the desert condition. Punishment is justified only where the one punished deserves to be subjected to coercion on grounds of culpable wrongdoing. So, one good reason to refrain from social punishing is that one is not in a position to really know what was done or how culpable the actor was. Further, among social equals in everyday life, we often cannot uncover the missing information. Privacy concerns may not permit us to inquire.

The desert condition in my account of punishment also limits the degree of coercive pressure to which a wrongdoer may be subjected. While informal social punishment aims at the wrongdoer's atonement, the theory does not allow punishers to apply coercion until the wrongdoer atones. If the wrongdoer remains unrepentant after we have applied a proportional amount of pressure, punishment must end.[25] The degree of pressure may not exceed the severity of the wrong or the wrongdoer's culpability. She only forfeits a degree of her liberty through her misdeed. Given that coercive social pressure tends to be cumulative in its effect, we should think of the degree of punishment in terms of what the wrongdoer receives, rather than what the punisher doles out. Again, even though a particular tweet condemning Justine is appropriate to her misdeed taken in itself, it is a disproportional punishment when Justine has already been targeted by a large number of similarly censuring tweets.

Interestingly, the harmfulness or coercive power of a particular act of social punishment depends on features of the context, including the relationships among the parties. Imagine my lunch companion treats a waitress with contemptuous impatience. After the waitress walks away,

---

[25] Of course, natural penalties may continue. The former punishers are free to choose to avoid the unrepentant wrongdoer simply in order to spend their time with more amiable companions.

I say, in a disapproving tone of voice, "You were really a jerk to her." If my lunch companion is a casual acquaintance, then my comment is quite aggressive. But if my lunch companion is my husband, then it probably is not. He might well receive it as Springer's type of moral criticism rather than as punishment. "Really? Do you think I was being unfair? She got our order wrong, after all." Avoiding my acquaintance's eye after such behavior might be just the right level of penalty for being rude to the waitress, whereas my husband would probably be quite hurt by my refusing to look him in the eye. In a close personal relationship, we have a legitimate expectation of contact, warmth, and cooperation, and so withholding that is harmful. At the same time, we expect loved ones to be more honest and forthcoming with us and take a greater interest in our behavior and character.

Similarly, in different cultures, the norms for criticizing and punishing vary. In some American cities, flashing a rude hand gesture at another driver is a routine form of social feedback. In other cities, it is seriously aggressive. I have seen strangers in Germany and Switzerland stop one another on the street to deliver lectures about violations of social rules, such as riding bicycles where it is not allowed or failing to clean up after one's dog. What would have been communicated with a dirty look in my hometown becomes a whole conversation. That I find the conversation more aggressive than the dirty look may be an effect of culture.

The instrumental condition in the moral pressure account requires that, in order to be justified, punishment must plausibly contribute to the goal of the wrongdoer making amends for her own misdeed. By directly pursuing this good, the punisher indirectly pursues other goods, including the maintenance of moral norms, the deterrence of wrongdoing, and the vindication of any victims of the wrongful action. The goal of the wrong-doer's atonement should affect our punishing practices in a number of ways.

For one thing, punishment is no longer justified if the wrongdoer has already atoned sufficiently for the wrong. In some cases, punishment should be suspended once the wrongdoer takes credible steps toward atonement. Blacklisting and gossip cannot be justified as forms of punishment because, taking place behind the wrongdoer's back, they play no direct role in encouraging atonement. One problematic aspect of the rhetoric of "canceling" a wrongdoer is that it seems to recommend permanently cutting off communications from the wrongdoer, as if her possible atonement could have no relevance for future relations. Presumably, though, what is canceled might be renewed.

Instrumental considerations might indicate that some people are better placed to impose informal social punishment than others. Wrongdoers may be more likely to respond appropriately to calls for atonement that come from the people they most esteem and trust.[26] In other cases, punishers who are perceived as being more objective than friends and family might be more effective.

Furthermore, methods of punishment that foreseeably undermine a wrongdoer's motivation or ability to atone are unjustified. Publicly shaming a wrongdoer frequently violates this principle. Shame is an emotion that tends to encourage hiding, passivity, and self-hatred rather than apology, reparation, and self-improvement. The difficulty of overcoming a loss of reputation might undermine a wrongdoer's motivation to make amends or her ability to reintegrate herself in the community. It might even drive her to despair. Similarly, if one knows that a particular person responds to any show of anger only with more anger and that her own impulse to defend herself prevents her from comprehending any moral message about her behavior, then rebukes and boycotts may not be good options. Other punitive methods, like social withdrawal, or nonpunitive methods such as moral persuasion may be preferable. Just because the wrongdoer deserves coercive interference, it does not follow that giving her what she deserves is the right thing to do.

Other instrumental considerations, in addition to our interest in the wrongdoer's atonement, also reasonably affect our choices about punishment. While encouraging a culpable wrongdoer to atone is a legitimate aim, it must be balanced against other legitimate goals and interests. Socially punishing a wrongdoer may indirectly harm other people, including victims and third parties. Potential punishers should consider whether their interference might undermine the ability of direct victims to stand up for themselves, or cause collateral damage to the relationships among wrongdoers, victims, and other members of the community. The parents of bullied children face just these sorts of problems. Young bullies both deserve to be interfered with and have a duty to make amends. But parents must balance the reasons for punishing the bully themselves with their duty to help their child learn to defend himself and regain the esteem of his classmates. The victim's parents must also respect the legitimate interests of the bully's parents and teachers in fulfilling their own duties, including their ability to build relationships of trust with the bully. Concerns about

---

[26] John Braithwaite, "Repentance Rituals and Restorative Justice," *Journal of Political Philosophy* 8, no. 1 (2000): 115–31.

backlashes and other unintended consequences can all be accommodated by the moral pressure theory of punishment.

In light of all of these risks of injustice and mischief, naming and shaming through social media looks like a particularly problematic method for informal social punishment. It is especially vulnerable to objections about determining guilt, punishing proportionately, avoiding unintended consequences, ulterior motives, and effectiveness in moving wrongdoers toward atonement and reintegration into in the community. Perhaps a good provisional rule is that informal social punishments should be delivered privately unless there is a good reason to punish publicly.[27] I return to this thought in Section 6, and consider what good reasons for public punishment might include.

5 THE AUTHORITY TO PUNISH

The discussion so far provides us with a number of reasons for believing that, in any particular case, only some people will be in a position to impose informal social punishment justly. Only some people will know whether the person acted wrongly, whether he has an excuse, and whether he has taken steps to make amends. Of those people, some will be better placed than others to punish in ways that are proportionate and constructive. In addition to these considerations, though, we should also consider whether some people simply lack the authority to punish particular kinds of wrongs.[28] For example, in the case of the young bully, one might argue that the victim's parents simply do not have the authority to punish someone else's child. They can recommend punishment to the bully's parents or teachers, but they cannot punish her themselves, even if they restrict themselves to standard methods of informal social punishment, such as rebuke. Similarly, one might argue that certain kinds of wrongdoing, like romantic infidelity, are no one's business but the two partners themselves. Mill argued (quite implausibly in my opinion) that self-harming behaviors are no one else's business and cannot be punished

---

[27] St. Thomas Aquinas defends a preference for private rebuke in *Summa Theologica*, trans. Fathers of the English Dominican Province, Project Gutenberg, 2006, 2a2ae, Q. 33, Art. 1–8. See also Michael Cook, *Commanding Right and Forbidding Wrong in Islamic Thought* (New York: Cambridge, 2000).

[28] J. R. Lucas, "Or Else," *Proceedings of the Aristotelian Society* 69 (1968): 207–22, at 212; and G. A. Cohen, "Casting the First Stone: Who Can, and Who Can't Condemn the Terrorists?," *Royal Institute of Philosophy Supplements* 81 (2006): 113–36.

either legally or socially.[29] Let's think of authority more generally as an entitlement to hold another person accountable.[30] The authority to punish is an entitlement to hold another person accountable via punishment, where punishment is otherwise justifiable.[31]

The question of authority is one I have been putting off for two chapters. But the time has come to consider it directly. Recall that I have defined punishment as authorized, intentional, reprobative, reactive harming. In the legal context, mob violence against a criminal is merely violence, not punishment, even if the criminal has been properly convicted. The mob lacks the entitlement to use force as a form of punishment. In the social context, someone who rebukes where it is not their business is merely meddling, not punishing.

Why should we believe that there is any such thing as the authority to punish? Why should we posit that an entitlement is present when one friend properly rebukes another or when a group of consumers legitimately boycotts a misbehaving corporation? The moral pressure theory already gives us a number of ways of talking about whether punitive acts like these are permissible or impermissible. We can appeal to considerations of desert. We can check whether punishment would lead to good consequences or not. Why also talk about authority?[32]

Well, one reason for including a concept of authority in our theory of informal social punishment is simply to preserve the parallel with theories of legal punishment, where authority is an established category. Another advantage is that it helps us distinguish informal social punishment from both legal punishment and formal social punishment. The differences include how entitlements to punish are distributed. These other two types of punishment are marked by asymmetrical forms of authority, while informal social punishment involves symmetrical authority. Friends have the right to hold one another accountable for things like failures of loyalty

---

[29] Mill, *On Liberty*, ch. I. Notice how extreme a position this is when it comes to social punishment. It entails that not even family members or close friends can use rebuke or social withdrawal in order to pressure loved ones to end self-destructive behaviors.

[30] Stephen Darwall, *The Second-Person Standpoint: Morality, Respect and Accountability* (Cambridge, MA: Harvard University Press, 2006). Elsewhere I have written referred to this concept as the "standing" to sanction (Linda Radzik, "On Minding Your Own Business: Differentiating Accountability Relations within the Moral Community," *Social Theory and Practice* 37, no. 4 (2011): 574–98). But a compelling argument that legal standing is the wrong analogy for what we are talking about here is presented by Marilyn Friedman, "How to Blame People Responsibly," *Journal of Value Inquiry* 47, no. 3 (2013): 275–82.

[31] Other ways to hold a person accountable include unexpressed moral judgments, unexpressed reactive attitudes, and moral criticism.

[32] Thanks to Timothy Schroeder and George Sher for raising this line of objection.

or caring. Each has an equal degree of authority to make legitimate demands of the other and enforce those demands. But within hierarchically structured social institutions like the state or the family, the entitlement to punish is restricted to specific institutional roles. Judges can fine citizens, but not vice versa. Parents can ground children, but not vice versa.

A theory of authority also helps us capture robust intuitions people have about informal social punishment. Sometimes, one person's rebuke of another person is inappropriate simply because the wrong in question is not her business. Even if the target of the rebuke is culpable, and even if the rebuke helps motivate the target to make amends, the rebuke is still unwarranted if the speaker is interfering in a situation that does not properly concern her. Similarly, an account of authority can help us explain why, in cases of hypocrisy and complicity, people who would normally be permitted to punish are not. Recall the chronically late person who cannot rebuke her friend for keeping her waiting. Or imagine one coworker who rebukes another for not finishing a project on time, when he himself contributed to unnecessary delays. Normally, friends and coworkers can rebuke lateness, but these two characters have lost their entitlement to hold their peers accountable.

These reflections help clarify what authority is and why we want to include it in our theory of punishment. But we also need an account of the basis of authority. Where does authority come from? Why do individuals have it in some situations but not others? This is a challenging question. I cannot present a full theory of authority here. But I would like to suggest that there are two general strategies for developing a plausible account of authority: a bottom-up strategy and a top-down strategy.

A bottom-up strategy grounds the authority to punish in particular, special relationships among people.[33] Consider, for example, relationships created through promises and other sorts of social contracts. If I promise to help you move next weekend, then this promise entitles you to hold me accountable in some way if I fail to fulfill my promise. If my failure is morally culpable and if, by punishing me, you can plausibly motivate me to make amends, then you may hold me accountable via punishment. Your entitlement to punish me is derived from the promise. Your neighbor

[33] T. M. Scanlon, *Moral Dimensions: Permissibility, Meaning, Blame* (Cambridge, MA: Belknap/ Harvard University Press, 2008), ch. 4; Garrath Williams, "Sharing Responsibility and Holding Responsible," *Journal of Applied Philosophy* 30, no. 4 (2013): 351–64; and Thomas Wilk, "Trust, Communities, and the Standing to Hold Accountable," *Kennedy Institute of Ethics Journal* 27, no. 2 supplement (2017): 1–22.

lacks the authority to punish me for the same wrong because she was not party to the promise.

Similarly, one might suggest that friends enter into a kind of social contract with one another in becoming friends, and that this contract gives each the right to enforce the various duties that are constitutive of friendship. Relationships that we find ourselves thrown into, like being someone's sibling, might also be a source of special duties and so a source of the authority to enforce such duties via informal social punishment.

The key advantage of the bottom-up strategy is that it yields an intuitively appealing account of why people generally should not intervene in other people's families and friendships. Coworkers should not refuse to collaborate with a fellow employee in order to punish him for committing adultery. His infidelity is between him and his spouse. Neighbors should not rebuke one another for their child-rearing choices because to do so would be to interfere in a relationship in which they are simply not a member. The bottom-up strategy may also be able to account for the intuition that one's own friends and family members would have the authority to punish wrongs one commits against third parties, since part of what we expect from family and friends is that they will help us make good decisions, encourage us to develop virtue, and sometimes even protect us from ourselves.

However, the bottom-up strategy runs into problems when special relationships of these sorts go severely wrong. It is not my business if my neighbors decide to homeschool their children rather than send them to public school. I may believe they are doing a disservice to the children. I may even be correct in that judgment. But it is their call to make. However, it *is* my business if the neighbors physically abuse their children. My coworker's infidelity may not be my business, but if I learn that he is recklessly exposing his spouse to sexually transmitted diseases, then I might well be entitled to intervene in some way, including by coercing him into telling his spouse by threatening to tell her myself.

If the authority to punish is always rooted in a special relationship, then it is not clear why outsiders are permitted to interfere when the special relationship becomes severely harmful. One might respond that, in these cases, the relevant relationship shifts. When the neighbors abuse their children, they are not only violating their special duties as parents, they are also violating a general moral duty – a duty all human beings have toward all other human beings. If that is the case, then, as a member of the human community, I may have the authority to punish them for abusing their children.

I take it that a bottom-up theorist will have to allow that the relationship of "fellow human beings" can ground the authority to punish in some cases anyway. Dealing properly with cases of human rights violations seems to require that move. Human rights violations are the sorts of things that are properly punished by anyone at all. Everyone has the authority to rebuke or socially withdraw from a murderer (though only the state can put her in prison).[34] It would surely be inappropriate to say, "I'm neither the victim nor a loved one, so it isn't my business." Some moral wrongs are surely everyone's business. But once we start thinking about people as fellow human beings – as fellow members of the moral community, or the Kingdom of Ends – then why would we not also have a legitimate interest in whether our fellow human beings are keeping their promises, raising their children well, and respecting their spouses? Yet once we take this step, authority no longer seems to be grounded in and limited to particular relationships; it is something universal.

This brings us to the second strategy for developing a theory of authority, the top-down approach. Here, we claim that the authority to hold people accountable for moral wrongdoing is universal – that everyone has the entitlement to punish any type of moral wrongdoing – but that this entitlement can be limited for specific, defeasible reasons. For example, everyone is entitled to punish lying, though a habitual liar typically forfeits her authority to do so.

While the suggestion that the authority to punish wrongdoing is universal might seem far-fetched at first, the idea has an impressive philosophical pedigree. John Locke's justification for the state seems to be built on such a premise.[35] In the state of nature, he argues, everyone has a natural right to retaliation and reparation. Everyone can punish wrongdoers and seize compensation, not only when they are themselves the victims of wrongdoing but also in defense of others. Locke argues that such a system leads to a number of inconveniences, including dangerous cycles of revenge. In order to avoid such inconveniences, individuals lay down a portion of their natural right to retaliation and reparation through a social contract that creates the state. But notice that the most plausible reading of Locke is that we lay down only a portion of this right. We cede only our right to punish wrongdoing through the application of force and violence.

---

[34] The social punishment of legal wrongs should still be subject to considerations of proportionality, though, as discussed in Section 4.
[35] John Locke, *Second Treatise of Civil Government* (Buffalo, NY: Prometheus Books, 1986). See also A. John Simmons, "Locke and the Right to Punish," *Philosophy and Public Affairs* 20 (1991): 311–49.

There is no reason to suppose that we lay down our right to punish via rebukes, cold shoulders, boycotting, or naming and shaming. Ceding all such powers to the state, and giving it jurisdiction over all the morally significant aspects of our lives, would create a new and dangerous set of problems.

Locke does not tell us much about nonlegal forms of punishment within the state, but one can imagine a Lockean theorist recommending further versions of social contracts under which we lay down our right to interfere in other people's romantic relationships, families, or friendships, except in cases where harms become severe. In this version of the top-down strategy, the authority to punish is universal – it is held by everyone over all types of moral wrongdoing – but then the authority is limited via mutually beneficial social contracts.

Mill provides us with a second version of a top-down strategy. He starts with an analysis of the concept of obligation. In *Utilitarianism*, he argues:

> We do not call anything wrong, unless we mean to imply that a person ought to be punished in some way or other for doing it.... It is a part of the notion of Duty in every one of its forms, that a person may rightfully be compelled to fulfil it. Duty is a thing which may be exacted from a person, as one exacts a debt. Unless we think that it may be exacted from him, we do not call it his duty.[36]

In other words, morally wrong actions are just those actions that can legitimately be punished. Who has the authority to punish? He tells us the wrongdoer should be punished "if not by law, by the opinion of his fellow-creatures; if not by opinion, by the reproaches of his own conscience."[37] What determines which of these parties – the state, the public, or the wrongdoer's own conscience – has the authority to punish in any particular case? Expediency.

> When we think that a person is bound in justice to do a thing, it is an ordinary form of language to say, that he ought to be compelled to do it. We should be gratified to see the obligation enforced by anybody who had the power. If we see that its enforcement by law would be inexpedient, we lament the impossibility, we consider the impunity given to injustice as an evil, and strive to make amends for it by bringing a strong expression of our own and the public disapprobation to bear upon the offender.[38]

Where social sanctions are impractical or too costly,

---

[36] John Stuart Mill, *Utilitarianism*, in *Collected Works of John Stuart Mill*, vol. 10, ed. J. M. Robson (Toronto: University of Toronto Press, 1969), V.14.
[37] Ibid.
[38] Ibid., V.13. See also Mill, *On Liberty*, I.11.

the conscience of the agent himself should step into the vacant judgment-seat, and protect those interests of others which have no external protection; judging himself all the more rigidly, because the case does not admit of his being made accountable to the judgment of his fellow creatures.[39]

If I am reading Mill correctly here, the authority to punish wrongdoing is universal in principle. Wrongdoing is everyone's business, but we limit the authority to punish in practice in order to maximize good consequences. In *On Liberty*, Mill provides an extended analysis of some of these consequences. The authority to punish is limited in the interest of personal liberty, individuality, and social progress.

In *The Second-Person Standpoint*, Stephen Darwall gives us a Kantian version of a top-down strategy for theorizing authority.[40] Darwall argues that to be a moral agent is to be the sort of being who can legitimately make demands of other people, and who can hold people accountable for failing to satisfy those demands. This form of authority is then intricately tied up with Darwall's account of moral obligation. Moral obligations are just those things that moral agents can authoritatively demand of one another as fellow members of the moral community. In other words, moral obligations just are those demands that everyone has the authority to enforce. Darwall does not draw clear distinctions among methods of holding people accountable in the *Second-Person Standpoint*, so it is not clear whether his theory of a universal and mutual authority to hold other people accountable is meant to imply a universal and mutual authority to socially punish wrongdoing, but one could certainly develop his theory in that direction.

There is a moment in Darwall's work where he notices that his theory seems to support people constantly interfering with one another.[41] He suggests that a Lockean social contract ceding of authority over certain areas of social life might be in order.[42] The top-down structure is clear: authority is universal in principle, but subject to restraint in practice for specific reasons. Reasons for restraining social punishment for certain kinds of wrongdoing that a Kantian can appreciate include things like respect for people's privacy and their interests in developing special relationships of trust and intimacy with friends and family, which are crucial

[39] Ibid.
[40] Darwall, *The Second-Person Standpoint*. I give a more detailed interpretation of Darwall's account of authority in Radzik, "On Minding Your Own Business."
[41] Stephen Darwall, "Reply to Korsgaard, Wallace and Watson," *Ethics* 118 (2007): 52–69, at 62n.
[42] Ibid.

to an agent's ability to develop her own conception of the right and the good.[43] Yet these special reasons for restricting the authority to punish particular kinds of wrongdoing could be outweighed by other interests more centrally related to agency, such as the interest the neighbor's children have in being free from physical abuse.

In this section, I have suggested two general strategies for making sense of the idea that some wrongs are simply not our business and so we are not entitled to punish them. I find the top-down strategy more promising than the bottom-up strategy. It does a better job of accommodating the fact that some wrongs are everyone's business, as well as the intuition that certain categories of wrongdoing (like poor parenting and infidelity) can shift from being not my business to my business based on the severity of the harms involved. I am also attracted to the conception of moral obligation that Mill and Darwall share. Moral duties just are those concerns that should matter to everyone. Whether or not you agree with me about the details, here, though, I hope to have made a compelling case for the claim that the authority to punish should be part of our theory of punishment. It is only one thread in our theory. One can have authority in a particular case and yet still punish without justification, if the desert and instrumental conditions are not met. But I believe thinking about authority as an independent factor is helpful.

6 THE CASE FOR NAMING AND SHAMING

In Section 4, I recommended a principle favoring private over public applications of informal social punishment. Private punishments, delivered from the punisher to the alleged wrongdoer out of the sight of a larger audience, seem to run fewer risks of punishing the guilty, insofar as it is easier for the accused to have their defenses heard. Private punishments avoid many of the dynamics that can feed into disproportional punishment. They may be more effective in motivating atonement, at least in most cases, and they present fewer obstacles to the wrongdoer's reintegration in the community. It is generally also easier to control unintended consequences in cases of private punishment. Ulterior motives may still be at play, but there may be less temptation to punish in order to signal one's own virtue, for example, when the wrongdoer is the punisher's only audience. Considerations of authority also seem to provide at least some

---

[43] Cf. Ferdinand David Schoeman, *Privacy and Social Freedom* (New York: Cambridge University Press, 1992).

support for a general preference for private punishment over public punishment. While I may have the proper authority to call my sister out for lying to me, or to pressure my close friend to stop ruining his health with alcohol, posting these rebukes on Facebook would recruit other parties, who may lack such authority, into the task of punishing.

A presumption in favor of private punishment is, of course, a presumption against naming and shaming on social media as a response to wrongdoing. Yet other reasons could outweigh the preference for punishing privately. Some of these suggest that the moral pressure theory that I have defended is too weak – that it fails to support some instances of informal social punishment that are intuitively justifiable.

In order to consider the case in favor of naming and shaming, I would like to reflect on the #MeToo campaign. At least many of the uses of the #MeToo hashtag fit our definitions of informal social punishment and naming and shaming. Another movement in the United States involves people reporting incidents of racial harassment on social media. In these cases, ordinary people (typically white) interfere with or call the police against black people who are going about everyday activities, such as (and these are real cases from 2018 alone): waiting for a business associate at a coffee shop, taking a nap in the common room of one's own college dormitory, picking up litter on the side of a road with a group of volunteers, mowing grass, and campaigning door-to-door for political office.[44] Such incidents have been publicized with another hashtag, #LivingWhileBlack, and variations such as #SleepingWhileBlack or #CampaigningWhileBlack. In some of these cases, the identities of the harassers have not been publicly revealed, but in other cases they have been.

There were two cases of #SwimmingWhileBlack in the summer of 2018 that I would like to describe in more detail. In one, a black mother and child entered a private pool club of which they were members by

---

[44] Rachel Siegel, "Two Black Men Arrested at Starbucks Settle with Philadelphia for $1 Each," *Washington Post*, online edition, May 3, 2018; Cleve R. Wootson Jr., "A Black Yale Student Fell Asleep in Her Dorm's Common Room. A White Student Called Police," *Washington Post*, online edition, May 11, 2018; Cleve R. Wootson Jr., "Add 'Performing Community Service while Black' to the List of Things That Make You Suspicious," *Washington Post*, online edition, May 15, 2018; Cleve R. Wootson Jr., "A White Woman Called Police on a Black 12-Year-Old – For Mowing Grass," *Washington Post*, online edition, June 30, 2018; and Kristine Phillips, "A Black Lawmaker Was Canvassing Door to Door in Her District. A Constituent Called 911," *Washington Post*, online edition, July 6, 2018.

virtue of living in the neighborhood and paying dues to a homeowners' association.[45] They were confronted by a white pool-goer, who was also the "pool chair" for the homeowners' association board. The mother was asked to show identification. She pointed out that no other pool-goers were being asked for ID, that there were no posted regulations requiring proof of residency, and that she could not have entered the pool complex in the first place without using a key. The police were called to resolve the dispute. In a second case, two black teenagers arrived at a pool, where they also had permission to be. They were immediately confronted by a white woman shouting, "Get out! Get out! Get out! Now!"[46] She threatened to call the police, used racial slurs, and even pushed and hit one boy. In both cases, the black pool-goers filmed the confrontations, and in both cases, the evidence supports their interpretations that they were being harassed because of their race. The videos went viral on social media. People who viewed the videos posted names and other identifying information about the harassers, including the names of their employers. Those employers came under pressure to respond to the incidents. In both cases, the wrongdoers were fired and their employers issued public statements declaring that these people had violated the values of the companies.[47]

In the #MeToo and the #LivingWhileBlack cases, public shaming may well have significant and long-lasting consequences for the wrongdoers, much like those suffered by Justine in our earlier example. The public shaming took place before very large audiences. Many people added their condemnations. The wrongdoers' family relationships and friendships have likely suffered quite a bit. They lost their jobs, and their professional and personal reputations are likely to remain tainted for a long time. Internet searches of their names will continually bring this information back to light, no matter what they might do to atone in the future.

Whether a punishment is overly severe depends on the severity of the wrong, of course. Some #MeToo cases involved very severe wrongs, including rape, with long-lasting consequences for victims. But in other cases, I suspect that many people will find the punishment disproportional to the wrong. Critics might also raise objections about differential punishment. Sadly, the #LivingWhileBlack incidents in which white people subject black people to unreasonable levels of suspicion and scrutiny are

---

[45] Alma McCarty, "'ID Adam': Man Who Questioned Black Woman's Right to Use Pool Loses Job," *USA Today*, online edition, July 7, 2018.

[46] Cleve R. Wootson Jr., "Police Say Woman Screamed Racial Slurs and Smacked a Black Teen at a Pool. She Lost Her Job," *Washington Post*, online edition, July 2, 2018.

[47] In the latter case, third-degree assault charges were also filed.

incredibly common. Some of the people having their lives upended by naming and shaming are only as guilty as a large portion of the white population of the United States, who go unpunished for their racism.

But we can also make a powerful case in favor of the #MeToo and #LivingWhileBlack public shaming campaigns. On the question of the authority to punish, sexism and racism are surely everyone's business. Oppression is a kind of injustice that persists because of ingrained cultural attitudes and entrenched structures of power. Both of these campaigns publicize forms of wrongdoing that have been condoned, minimized, or ignored for literally centuries.

#MeToo was inspired by the fact that women who report sexual misconduct have generally not been treated as credible.[48] There are often no third-party witnesses to such transgressions. Complaints are also frequently dismissed or downplayed because the interests of the accused in maintaining his reputation and his position in the community are weighed more heavily than the interests of the victim. #MeToo has gone a long way toward raising public awareness of the frequency and the harmfulness of sexual assault and harassment.

Similarly, the overpolicing and harassment of black people is a widespread and underacknowledged problem. Oversurveillance pervades all aspects of black people's lives in the United States and the psychological and social consequences accumulate over time. Too often, contact with the police is life-threatening for black Americans. The #LivingWhileBlack hashtag, and especially the videos that vividly document harassment and abuse, provide powerful and broadly accessible forms of evidence of antiblack racism in everyday life.[49]

Furthermore, many of the types of wrongs to which the #MeToo and #LivingWhileBlack campaigns respond are not handled well by the legal system. Racist speech is not illegal in the United States. Formulating an effective law to stop white people from calling the police for absurd reasons would likely prove difficult. Bias, harassment, and sexual assault are notoriously hard to prove in criminal and civil courts. Victims often find

---

[48] Emily Shugerman, "Me Too: Why Are Women Sharing Stories of Sexual Assault and How Did It Start?," *Independent*, online edition, October 17, 2017.

[49] Research on American public opinion suggests that white people believe that racial bias *against white people* is more prevalent than bias against black people. Michael I. Norton and Samuel R. Sommers, "Whites See Racism as a Zero-Sum Game That They Are Now Losing," *Perspectives on Psychological Science* 6, no. 3 (2011): 215–18. Such research may well be evidence for both the importance of consciousness-raising efforts like #LivingWhileBlack and the backlash against such efforts.

legal proceedings traumatizing. These considerations strengthen the case for mobilizing burdensome forms of social punishment, including public shaming.

The moral pressure theory argues that the proper aim of informal social punishment is to pressure culpable wrongdoers to make amends for their own misdeeds. I have argued that this goal encompasses many other worthy instrumental ends. But the #MeToo and #LivingWhile-Black campaigns suggest that these other ends of punishment might outweigh the importance of the wrongdoer's atonement and might even justify methods of punishment that tend to undermine atonement. These other ends include the deterrence of wrongdoing, the vindication of the victims of wrongdoing, and the maintenance and promulgation of moral norms.

We have here a classic conflict between desert-based and instrumental arguments for punishment. The public shaming of a relatively small number of perpetrators of racial and sexual harassment could have a large, positive impact going forward. But such punishments threaten to punish disproportionately and may well be counterproductive to the wrongdoer's atonement, thereby treating the one punished as a mere means to the well-being of other people.

I am enough of a deontologist to emphasize the importance of respecting wrongdoers. #MeToo and #LivingWhileBlack posts might still make important contributions while shielding the identity of the wrongdoer. For example, videos that blur the faces of offenders while capturing their words and gestures would provide some measure of deterrence while supporting victims and promulgating norms. Wrongdoers would likely experience such posts as shaming because they would still be identifiable to the members of their close social circles, but as less damaging than when their identities are fully revealed to the public at large.

However, I am not so extreme a deontologist as to claim that the interests of the many never outweigh the interests of the few. Sometimes publicly revealing the identities of wrongdoers may be the only way to prevent them from continuing to harm other people or to press the police, universities, or employers to take accusations of abuse and harassment seriously. Sometimes making a public example of a small number of culpable wrongdoers in the name of a greater good might be the best thing to do all things considered. After all, wrongdoers themselves always have the choice to use the experience as a step toward atonement. Instances of wrongdoing that are symptomatic of entrenched forms of oppression, like those targeted by the #MeToo and

#LivingWhileBlack campaigns, are good candidates for such exceptions to our usual standards for punishment.

7 CONCLUSION

As I mentioned in Chapter 1, I am not a fan of punishment in general, nor am I recommending an increase in the use of informal social punishment in particular. However, I have argued that it can be both a permissible and a constructive way to hold people responsible for their actions. I have argued that our practices should be both aimed at and limited by the wrongdoer's atonement, and that informal social punishments are generally better delivered in private rather than in public. But each of these claims is defeasible. I am aware that this book raises as many questions as it answers. I hope that other scholars will take up these issues, as Christopher Bennett, George Sher, and Glen Pettigrove do in the next three chapters.

In hopes of encouraging such scholarship, let me point toward some further questions about social punishment that need to be addressed. When is informal social punishment not merely permissible but also obligatory? What factors should affect the choice between private and public punishment? Does it matter if the wrongdoer is a public figure or not? Does it matter whether the wrong was witnessed by an audience or not? The relationship between legal and social punishment also needs further consideration. Should the fact that criminals tend to be subjected to social punishment influence criminal sentencing practices? Which kinds of wrongdoing can be punished by an employer or a university, and which lie beyond the scope of their authority or competence? Is it permissible to fire employees for transgressions unrelated to their jobs, and if so, when? Should universities be expected to adjudicate charges of rape on campus, rather than leaving them to the state?[50] Do people ever have a moral right to do wrong?[51] If so, what sorts of protections would such a right guarantee? For example, should a moral right to participate in politics protect business owners from being boycotted over donations to controversial candidates or causes, or government officials from being refused service by private

---

[50] Sarah L. Swan, "Between Title IX and the Criminal Law: Bringing Tort Law to the Campus Sexual Assault Debate," *Kansas Law Review* 64, no. 4 (2016): 963–86.

[51] See Jeremy Waldron, "A Right to Do Wrong," *Ethics* 92, no. 1 (1981): 21–39; and William A. Galston, "On the Alleged Right to Do Wrong: A Response to Waldron," *Ethics* 93 (1983): 320–24.

businesses for implementing objectionable policies?[52] Or are such methods of informal social punishment permissible ways of enforcing respect for moral standards in political activities?

Each of these questions is made more pressing by the turbulent and politically divisive times we find ourselves in today. Informal social punishment has always been a tool of social control. It has always been used both for good and for ill. But social media has amplified the power of informal social punishment considerably. It is time to talk about how this power should be used.

[52] Mary Jordan, "The Latest Sign of Political Divide: Shaming and Shunning Public Officials," *Washington Post*, online edition, June 24, 2018.

PART II

Commentaries

CHAPTER 4

How to Do Things with Blame (and Social Punishment)

Christopher Bennett

In this response I deal with issues raised by the first chapter of Linda Radzik's wonderful account of social punishment. Radzik's acute and stimulating discussion engages with an important and underexplored topic and, in my opinion, makes a convincing case that punishment does not only happen when it is meted out by the state. However, from this well-argued point she goes on to cast the net of 'social punishment' significantly wider: for instance, claiming that rebukes can and often should be seen as punishments. On this point I am less clear. However, because I do not want the dispute to be a merely verbal one, my aim in this response is to draw out what is at issue when we disagree over whether something should be classed as punishment. Having set out the key parts of Radzik's position (Sections 1 and 2) and registered some concerns that I have about it (Sections 3–6), I set out a taxonomy of things that we can do with blame or social punishment (Sections 7 and 8), aiming to show why we might have reason to put different kinds of responses into different categories. Which of these categories we decide to call 'punishment' does not matter too much as long as we are clear on the underlying differences between these types of response, and the different types of challenge they set us in any attempt to justify or practice them.

I RADZIK ON INFORMAL SOCIAL PUNISHMENT

In Chapter 1, "Defining Social Punishment," Linda Radzik is concerned to show that the phenomenon of punishment is not confined to the sphere of formal statutory criminal justice and that something that can be called 'social punishment' is carried out quite commonly within interpersonal relations. Her particular interest, however, is not in 'formal social punishment,' by which she means sanctions imposed by nonstatutory authorities such as parents, employers, and teachers, but rather in 'informal social punishment.' Informal social punishment can include angry and sarcastic

75

remarks, shunning the person, or leaving them out, doled out "among social equals."[1] Following Mill in describing this as the "moral coercion of public opinion," she declares herself to be ambivalent about the justification of informal social punishment (we hear more about this in the other two lectures), but convinced of the importance of recognizing and theorizing about it.

Radzik gives a number of examples of the kind of thing she claims to be informal social punishment, drawn from advice columnist Carolyn Hax. For instance, a woman depriving her parents-in-law of contact with their grandchildren as a punishment for their lack of interest in her as a person. A brother punishing his sister by withdrawing from her emotionally for telling a lie with the selfish and jealous intention of ruining his relationship. A person punishing another, again by emotional withdrawal, for blithely asking about a holiday that, apparently, she should have known to have been ruined by a miscarriage. Radzik also mentions a case of punishment by the pains of conscience – however, I will take it that the paradigm of the phenomenon she is interested in is provided by the first three cases, and is interpersonal rather than intrapersonal. The key thing is that Radzik presents some nice examples of our use of the term 'punishment' to describe things that are not imposed by any statutory authority, and she wants to argue that such usage is not merely metaphorical: she argues that there is a perfectly straightforward connection between these responses and more formal, institutional punishments.

Not resting with this intuitive appeal to the naturalness and apparent nonmetaphorical nature of such idioms, Radzik's main argumentative strategy in this lecture is to take a standard definition of punishment and to show that each of its elements is met in informal social punishment. According to Radzik, this standard definition takes punishment to be *authorized, intentional, reprobative, reactive harming.*[2] From her use of this strategy to show informal social punishment to be punishment, I infer that Radzik takes these elements to be individually necessary and jointly sufficient conditions of something counting as punishment. As long as some action meets these conditions, in other words, this is sufficient to show that the action is punishment. Now it seems clear that there will be many cases of *formal* social punishment that meet these conditions: for instance, where a parent sends a child to their bedroom for bullying their younger sibling. Here the parent can be thought to have something like

[1] Linda Radzik, Chapter 1 in this volume, 12.
[2] Ibid., 3.

fiduciary authority over the child that makes it intelligible for them to claim a right to punish the child. The act is a response to the bullying (reactive condition) which expresses disapproval (reprobative condition). Sending the child to their bedroom is different from simply telling them it is time for bed and is hence a deprivation of some good or freedom that the child could otherwise have expected to enjoy (harm condition). And the act is intentional in a number of senses – the sending to the room is an intentional act; the act is intended as the imposition of a deprivation; and the imposition of a deprivation is intended as a reprobative response to the wrongdoing. We might also add, in this case, that there is likely to be an intention that the child should recognize that they are being sent to their room, not because it is time for bed, but because they are being punished. Radzik is correct, then, to say that it is not necessary to punishment that it be a response to infractions of *legal* rules. The question is whether there are interesting examples of things that we do informally in response to such infractions that can also be thought of as punishments.

As Radzik sets this up, it is the question of whether punishments can be imposed, not only in the context of hierarchically structured institutional relationships but also between social equals. Her argument is that one thing that can often take place between such social equals is rebuke, and that rebukes are, or can often be, punishments, in virtue of their meeting the conditions given in the definition we have just looked at. She defines rebuke as "an overt expression of disapproval, through words or gestures, addressed to a perceived transgressor, that both attributes responsibility to her for a transgression and expresses some form of anger, such as resentment or indignation."[3] She claims that not all rebukes are punishments (seemingly because they don't always meet the intention condition: sometimes we "cannot help but roll [our] eyes"[4]), but that they often are.

2 THE ELEMENTS OF PUNISHMENT IN INFORMAL SOCIAL PUNISHMENT

Radzik's strategy to support the conclusion that rebukes are informal social punishment is to take each of the elements in the definition of punishment in turn and to argue that they are each present in rebukes. Let me run through some of her arguments quickly, since these will be important for what I have to say later on. Her first topic is the harm condition. Radzik

[3] Ibid., 12.
[4] Ibid.

argues that rebukes should be distinguished from "moral criticism," which
simply involves "communications that call another person's attention to a
moral concern" (where she presumably intends a "moral concern" to
signify not just something we take to be of moral importance but something in that person's attitudes or conduct that we purportedly have reason
to be *worried* about morally speaking).[5] Rebukes, she thinks, have a
"harder edge" to them.[6] I take it that the distinction here is that moral
criticism always implies a judgment that a person should think again about
their conduct and attitude, whereas rebukes, as Radzik says, "subject" a
person to one's anger, or "target" that anger *at* the person, and if they
communicate a message to the person being blamed, it is not simply that
they should think again, but also that "*you* are angry with him."[7]

Radzik then moves on to the reprobative, reactive, and intention
conditions. She treats it as uncontroversial that rebuke must be an expression of disapproval in response to some transgression, thus meeting the
first two conditions. In dealing with intention, it is not enough that there
be an intention to cause harm: Radzik is clear that it is an intention to
impose harm *as a response to the offense* that is the key thing. She says:

When the brother addresses angry words to his sister, when he tells her just how
despicable her lie was, he knows that she will find this unpleasant. This is part of
his point in telling her off. He wants her to feel bad. If she does not feel bad, if she
remains cool and unmoved, then his purpose is frustrated.[8]

Now one way of understanding what Radzik has in mind here is that the
brother's purpose is to get his sister to recognize, confront, and 'take
ownership of' the despicable nature of her action, and that he intends this
even though he understands that her feeling terrible about herself is a
necessary concomitant of coming to such an understanding. In such a case
we may well say that he intends her to feel bad for what she has done.
However, one reason for thinking that Radzik has something else in mind
is that one might have this intention even though one delivers only "moral
criticism" rather than a harder-edged rebuke. As Radzik says:

Calmly stating a moral claim, or attempting to persuade an offender with a cool
display of moral reasoning, is significantly different from angrily confronting or
coldly shunning that person. Rebukes and cold shoulders send their moral
message to the offender by knowingly and purposefully subjecting him to hard

---

[5] Ibid., 13.
[6] Ibid.
[7] Ibid.
[8] Ibid., 16.

treatment. In this way, the standard definition of punishment also helps us to draw a distinction between socially punishing and merely expressing blame. Overtly blaming is an intentionally reprobative reaction to a transgression. It might even be experienced as harmful by the target, who may feel exposed or humiliated. But merely blaming does not intentionally (i.e., knowingly and purposely) impose a harm.[9]

For the reasons just given, I think Radzik is wrong to say that in overt blame we do not know and intend that it will make the person confront what they have done, and hence cause them to feel bad about themselves. Even in this case there can be an intention to harm, in Radzik's terms. However, if we want to know what harm she takes to be intended in rebuke, it sounds as though she is imagining a rebuke to involve something more *immediately* unpleasant to experience. The intention in rebuking is therefore to impose a harm – to impose "hard treatment," as she puts it here – in the sense that one intends to make it unpleasant to the person that they have to hear you out. For this to be different from what we have just said about overt blame, the unpleasantness must not lie in the *content* of what you have to say so much as in the *mode of its delivery*. As she suggests in the definition of rebuke that I quoted earlier, the key thing that distinguishes rebuke from overt blame is the presence and expression of emotion, presumably of the sort that Hume called violent rather than calm passions and, in particular, anger, resentment, and indignation. Therefore, what she talks about as the hard treatment involved in rebuke must have to do with being subjected to another's irritation, or anger, or rage. It is this that she claims is enough to meet the harm condition in punishment.

Regarding the authorization condition, Radzik argues that authorization is indeed required for informal social punishment, and that it therefore fits the standard definition on this point also, but that we should not think of authority in the same way as in legal punishment. We should not think of the authority necessary for informal social punishment as the kind of authority that is asymmetrically held in a hierarchically structured rela-tionship. Rather, authority can be held by social equals. But we can see that authority is necessary for informal social punishment, Radzik claims, from the fact that the right to engage in informal social punishment can be defeated by a justified charge that it is not one's business (and hence, we might add, that one is operating outside one's *jurisdiction* or sphere of authority) or a justified charge of hypocrisy (and hence, we might add, that one has *forfeited* one's authority with respect to this domain).

---

[9] Ibid., 18.

3 A PROBLEM WITH RADZIK'S USE OF THE DEFINITION
OF PUNISHMENT

Having set out Radzik's main argumentative strategy, I now turn to some problems with it. Let us begin with the reactive, reprobative, and intention conditions. While, as Radzik notes, a rebuke is clearly reactive and reprobative – it is a form of response to an infraction that communicates disapproval of that infraction – I do not think that this is enough to establish that it is reactive and reprobative *in the same way as punishment*. And I think that this shows a problem with her argumentative strategy of using the elements of the definition to make her case. To illustrate my concern, let us look at the distinction that, following Mill, she draws between social punishment and "natural penalties."[10] A natural penalty involves harming someone. It involves foreseeably and perhaps even intentionally harming a person: for instance, by withdrawing one's company from them and perhaps encouraging others to do so. Now harming a person in this way is something one does for reasons, and these will often be reasons for finding the person uncongenial or unpleasant: one finds the person to be (let us say) boring or smelly or to drink too much. Now Radzik wants to argue that we can see how natural penalties differ from social punishments by appeal to the definition of punishment: we can see, she thinks, that natural penalties, although they may be in some sense intentional, are not reactive or reprobative harming. Not so fast, however. After all, when I inflict a natural penalty on someone, I do so because of something in them of which I disapprove (I disapprove of it at least in the sense that I do not want to associate with people who have those features if I can help it). The judgment of disapproval is in some sense *expressed* in my avoidance of them, since I avoid them consciously for that reason: my attitude is, we might say, manifested in my action. But if this point is correct, then it looks as though the reactive and reprobative conditions are met *in some sense*. Furthermore, I act intentionally in avoiding this person. Therefore, in order to draw the distinction between such penalties and social punishments, we need to be more specific about the kind of response to features we disapprove of that is distinctive of punishment – or of what it means for punishment to *express* disapproval.

Now one thing we might say is that in natural penalties the disapproval is implied, whereas in social punishment it is made explicit. However, this

---

[10] Ibid., 16.

is not quite enough. Imagine that my alcoholic friend asks why I have been avoiding him, and under conversational pressure I explain to him why. After this event I persist in my policy of avoiding him. Now my judgment has been made explicit. However, that does not mean that I am now punishing him for his alcoholism. Rather, I am avoiding him because that is not how I want to spend my life. Thus, it must be the case that punishment makes the attitude of disapproval explicit *in a particular way*. But in what way, exactly? Radzik explains this by means of the following distinction:

Mill says you are permitted to avoid [this] person but not to parade your avoidance. You can knowingly harm him, but you cannot purposefully harm him as a reprobative response to his actions or character. The purposeful expression of a message of disapproval turns social avoidance from a case of merely minding your own business to a case of social punishment.[11]

What I take Radzik to have in mind here is that in social punishment the avoidance is adopted *specifically* in order to give voice to one's disapproval – where one's purpose in avoiding the person is to convey that one disapproves. However, this shows that it is not enough, for something to be punishment, that it be an intentional harmful response that conveys disapproval. It must be that the agent engages in that response *because* the harming of that person conveys disapproval, or perhaps *in order to* convey disapproval.

This shows a problem with Radzik's strategy. She takes a definition of punishment which gives conditions that she treats as individually necessary and jointly sufficient. That she treats them as jointly sufficient is shown by her argument that rebukes are punishment in virtue of meeting those conditions. However, I have argued that simply meeting these conditions is *not* enough for something to be punishment. For "natural penalties," which Radzik agrees are not punishments, can be seen to meet these conditions. If these conditions are to be seen as jointly sufficient, then, we must pay attention to the *specific* way in which these conditions are *combined* in punishment, and the sense that these definitional terms have when so combined. Separating them out, in the way Radzik's strategy does, runs the risk of allowing us to forget that for something to be punishment it has to be "reactive," "reprobative," and "harmful" *in a certain way*, and be governed by an "intention" *of a distinctive sort*. Each of these jointly sufficient conditions is only an *aspect* of a distinctive unified

---

[11] Ibid., 17.

phenomenon, punishment, in which they are combined in a specific way. Therefore, showing that rebukes are reactive and reprobative does not, as Radzik thinks, thereby establish that they are punishments. It would also have to be shown that they are reactive and reprobative in the same way as paradigm cases of punishment.

4 ARE REBUKES REACTIVE AND REPROBATIVE IN THE SAME WAY AS PUNISHMENT?

The conclusion from the previous section is that, for Radzik's strategy to succeed, we need to show (a) in what way punishment is intentional, harmful, reactive, reprobative, and authorized and then (b) that rebukes are intentional, harmful, reactive, reprobative, and authorized in the same, or a sufficiently close, sense. Now rebukes are clearly less like natural penalties, and closer to what we have said about punishments, since they are things we engage in for the purposes of conveying disapproval. However, this is not enough to make them punishment, on Radzik's view, since some forms of overt blame and moral criticism can also be engaged in for the purpose of conveying disapproval, and Radzik rightly denies that such cases would be social punishment. As we saw above, one difference between the two is that in social punishment one has a further intention, the intention that the target of punishment should be harmed, or made to suffer something unpleasant, or made to feel bad. However, while Radzik thinks of rebukes as moral criticism with a "harder edge," she should agree that one cannot make moral criticism into punishment simply by doing something that a person will find unpleasant at the same time as criticizing them. Punishment is not simply moral criticism *plus* hard treatment. Rather, punishment involves conveying disapproval *through* doing something unpleasant to someone. To repeat what Radzik herself says in distinguishing social punishment from overt blame: "Rebukes and cold shoulders send their moral message to the offender by knowingly and purposefully subjecting him to hard treatment."[12] One treats them in a way that they will find unpleasant with the purpose of *thereby* conveying disapproval of that wrongdoing.

We should conclude, therefore, that it is essential to punishment that hard treatment is imposed *thereby* to convey disapproval, and this helps us to understand not just what the elements in the definition of

---

[12] Ibid., 18.

punishment should be, but how they are to be combined. However, we can still press for more clarity on *how* they are to be combined. One interpretation would be that it is sufficient for something to be a case of punishment that disapproval be conveyed through hard treatment in the sense that a message is made more hard-hitting, and hence more likely to be understood or acknowledged, by the imposition of hard treatment. On this interpretation, an act of moral criticism would be punishment as long as it involved some unpleasant treatment to ram the point home. Now it may be that this is the view that underpins Radzik's claim that rebukes are punishments. However, I am not convinced. Let me illustrate the concern by returning to the examples of 'punishment' that Radzik draws from Carolyn Hax. While I am not entirely convinced that the description of these cases as 'punishments' is literal rather than metaphorical, I don't find it entirely unintuitive to think of them in that way. But intuitively I would not describe these cases as rebukes, or at least not all of them. Whereas 'rebuke' connotes angry engagement with a perceived wrongdoer, in which verbal expression of disapproval is an essential element, these cases involve intentional nonverbalized *disengagement*. Furthermore, in at least one case (the parents-in-law one) the behavior does not seem to be addressed to the recipients at all, and certainly not as something the woman intends her parents-in-law to understand as an expression of disapproval. (This is not necessarily to say that there is no sense in which it expresses disapproval, simply that it does not aim to express that disapproval *to them*.) The reason I think it may be plausible to describe the withdrawal cases as punishments, however, is because, like punishments, they involve a form of behavior toward a perceived wrongdoer that is such as to *mark* their behavior as wrongful. Insofar as withdrawal in the Hax cases figures as the 'harm' element in Radzik's definition of punishment, what is distinctive of punishment is that the harm or withdrawal is the *vehicle* of the expression of disapproval in the sense that the harming conduct *means* disapproval, independently of whether it is accompanied by verbal expression of disapproval. Withdrawal means or is expressive of disapproval in the way that kneeling in church means or is expressive of awe in the presence of a being of incomparable worth. However, this suggests a different interpretation of the thought that in punishment disapproval is conveyed through hard treatment. It is not just that it makes the disapproval more hard-hitting: for it to be punishment, it must be that the hard treatment has taken on a different meaning, that it *stands for* or *embodies* or *externalizes* the attitude of disapproval in the way that kneeling in church stands for or externalizes the sense of awe.[13] I return to this point in Sections 7 and 8 below.

If this is the case, how should we think about whether rebukes are reactive and reprobative in the way that punishments are? It will depend on whether the treatment involved in subjecting someone to one's anger is such as to *mean* disapproval in the way that withdrawal means disapproval. Perhaps this is plausible. For instance, angry treatment of a wrongdoer can be such as to violate normally robust interpersonal boundaries of care and respect (e.g., when in anger one 'gets in someone's face'). Perhaps such angry treatment means or stands for disapproval of the way in which the wrongdoer acted as though such interpersonal boundaries were not limits to their own action. However, I will not broach this question further at present. It is clear, though, that Radzik does not provide an argument to show that rebukes express disapproval *in the way that* punishments express disapproval, since she does not distinguish between different ways in which emotion, hard treatment, and disapproval may be combined. Radzik's lecture draws attention to an interesting and important set of questions. But their answer is more complex than she allows because punishment is a more complex phenomenon than her definition suggests. This may be one reason why there is a notorious 'problem of punishment' rather than a 'problem of expressing anger'.[14]

Radzik might object that my argument has all taken place on the shifting sands of intuition. I agree that we need more than this. I think what we need is a taxonomy of different kinds of reaction to wrongdoing that we have reason to distinguish. Giving such a taxonomy will help us to see what, for example, social punishment is by helping us to see what it is not; but it will also help us to see what value there might be in the fact that our practice draws certain conceptual distinctions and upholds certain categorizations. To this end, I will discuss the range of things we can do in the way of criticizing, expressing disapproval, expressing emotion, blaming, and informally punishing, in the closing sections of this essay. However, before we get to that, we need to look at what Radzik says about the harm and authority conditions.

---

[13] For more on the conception of expression invoked here, see my "Expressive Actions," in *The Expression of Emotion*, ed. C. Abell and J. Smith (Cambridge: Cambridge University Press, 2016), 73–94.
[14] Though, of course, expressions of anger can also be controversial. See, e.g., Amia Srinivasan, "The Aptness of Anger," *Journal of Political Philosophy* 26, no. 2 (2018): 123–44.

5 DO REBUKES HARM IN THE WAY THAT PUNISHMENTS DO?

As we have seen, Radzik thinks that rebukes cause harm in the sense that it is unpleasant to be subjected to someone's anger. But is this the kind of harm involved in punishment? Radzik argues against one purported reason to doubt that it is, which is David Shoemaker's claim that rebuke is not punishment since it does not involve "depriving you of anything to which you would otherwise have rights."[15] On Shoemaker's line of criticism, rebuke simply involves 'saying' things rather than 'doing' things. Radzik's response to this is to argue that Shoemaker sets the bar too high if he is talking about (fundamental) moral or legal rights, since these are likely implicated only in cases of serious, normally legal punishment, and that if his view were correct he would not even be able to accommodate formal social punishments like the parent sending the child to their room. However, I think this response, while correct as far as it goes, misses the mark. Take the example above of the child being sent to their room. In explaining why that example plausibly involves punishment, I did not say that the parents aim to harm their child. It seemed more natural to say that it involves depriving the child of goods or freedoms that they could otherwise have reasonably expected to enjoy. I think it *may* indeed be a stretch to say that the child is harmed by being sent to their room – after all, this is what normally happens to the child at bedtime, and is not harmful then. But whether or not that is correct, I think we can talk about the child having, if not *rights* to certain goods and freedoms, then at least reasonable normative expectations, or perhaps even entitlements, regarding these goods and freedoms that are suspended in the punishment. Furthermore, Shoemaker's claim also fits the Hax cases involving emotional withdrawal – in these cases the 'punisher' withdraws some contact or closeness that the 'punished' would otherwise, given their relationship, have some entitlement to expect. If Shoemaker's claim is understood as being about fundamental moral rights, then I agree that it is not plausible – but I don't see why it needs to be so understood. Hence, I don't think Radzik has a good response to someone who insists that the harm involved in punishment has to involve a deprivation of something (a good, or a form of treatment) that the punished party would otherwise have some kind of normative expectation of enjoying.

---

[15] David Shoemaker, "Blame and Punishment," in *Blame: Its Nature and Norms*, ed. D. Justin Coates and Neal A. Tognazzini (New York: Oxford University Press, 2013), 100–118.

Another reason for doubting that the 'harm' condition Radzik has in mind is adequate is that we cannot see something as a punishment if it simply involves imposing some entirely undifferentiated harm on a person in response to a crime.[16] This is another example in which Radzik's method of separating out the elements of punishment and treating them in isolation from one another leads her astray. And it relates to the condition that we saw in our discussion of the reactive and reprobative conditions: that in punishment the hard treatment *means* disapproval. Punishment has in some way to fit the crime – this is not just a moral desideratum but a condition of its intelligibility as punishment. It is not punishment, that is, unless we see the harm or deprivation as in some way intelligibly related to the crime in such a way as to mean disapproval of it. Shoemaker's view that punishment involves a deprivation of normal treatment meets that intelligible connection condition since such a punishment reflects the offender's own departure from due treatment. Radzik might argue that attempting to harm someone by making them feel bad for what they have done also meets such an intelligibility condition. I would agree with that – at least if she is interpreted to mean feeling *morally* bad. However, I also think that a promising line of response against Shoemaker's claim that rebukes are not punishments would have been for Radzik to argue that rebukes *do* deprive someone of something to which they have a right, namely, respect and concern. After all, respect and concern plausibly involve some (defeasible) entitlements to positive treatment, but also (defeasible) entitlements that others refrain from attempting intentionally to make them feel fundamentally bad about themselves, for instance, as in ridicule or humiliation. The possibility of deserved rebuke would be a limited, focused exception to this normal entitlement: the person is deprived of respect and concern in a certain respect, namely, with regard to the conduct for which they are being rebuked and the personal traits that led to it. Another limited, focused exception might be rights to freedom of speech – a controversial case of which would be the ridicule to which Muslims have been subjected by Danish and French cartoonists. But these examples show only that there are exceptions to entitlements to respect and concern, not that there are no such entitlements. Contra Shoemaker, rebukes do not just involve saying things; they also involve doing things, and they can have significant psychological effects.

---

[16] For more on this theme, see my "The Varieties of Retributive Experience," *Philosophical Quarterly* 52, no. 207 (2002): 145–63.

6 DO REBUKES REQUIRE AUTHORITY IN THE SAME WAY PUNISHMENT DOES?

Radzik argues that informal social punishment is a form of punishment in that it does require authority, but that the authority in question does not have to be asymmetric and hierarchical. However, it seems to me that she accepts too quickly that informal social punishment can only be punishment if it meets the authority condition. After all, given that she is explicitly dealing with informal social punishment, it might have made sense for Radzik to argue that the authority condition is only necessary when punishment is formal. Why does she not consider the possibility that the authority condition need only be a condition of formal punishment? One answer might be that her strategy of working from the definition requires her to accept the authority condition. But that is not convincing, since nothing requires her to accept the elements of that definition uncritically. Another answer might be that she is convinced that informal social punishment can be defeated by credible accusations of hypocrisy or 'none of your business' and that she thinks that this shows that authority is involved. However, even if she is right to be convinced about this, the question is whether it shows that the authority involved in rebukes is the same, or of a sufficiently closely related sort, to that involved in punishment. And it might seem that there are at least some important reasons for thinking that it is not, and that in talking about the authority to rebuke Radzik has changed the subject. Let us see how that case might be made.

In the case of formal punishment, the argument might go, a given agent claims a right to punish *because* it also claims rights to legislate for subjects, that is, to set standards for permissible conduct or to provide further determinations of independently existing standards of permissible conduct.[17] This is the case for states, but also for authorities in formal social punishment, such as parents or employers. Parents have the authority to punish their children, but children do not have authority to punish one another – not in the same sense. This is because even if parents do not explicitly legislate for their children, they claim the final say on what counts as 'just fun' and what counts as bullying. Parents and employees can claim a right to punish because they have a right to hold those subject to their legislation to account to the standards that they have laid down for them. Formal punishment requires authority, therefore, because it is the

---

[17] For some more on the line of argument explored in this paragraph, see my "The Authority of Moral Oversight," *Legal Theory* 25, no. 3 (2019): 153–77.

'enforcement' aspect of a complex right that the punishing agent claims to have to legislate standards, to adjudicate on whether those standards have been met, and to hold subjects accountable when they have not met them. To put this differently, we might say that the kind of authority involved in legal punishment involves a complex Hohfeldian power, that is, a normative ability to change subjects' rights and obligations by determining, adjudicating, and enforcing standards. This power may sometimes be thought of as a purely legal power, that is, one that is justified by purely legal provisions and that alters purely legal rights and obligations. But the more interesting case is that in which it can be thought of as a *normative power*, which is justified by normative provisions and which alters nonlegal rights and obligations.[18] This is presumably how parents are thinking of it when they claim a right, not held by other adults, to punish their own children. It is the fact that punishment is here the enforcement part of this complex power that marks it out as formal punishment.

However, if this is right, then when Radzik insists that authority is present in informal social punishment she must be talking about a different sense of authority. At any rate, she does not put forward an argument to the effect that social equals do have a Lockean right, as individuals, to legislate for one another and adjudicate and enforce that legislation. Rather, her argument regarding the authority condition takes a different strategy. The considerations on which Radzik draws are sometimes characterized not in terms of authority but rather 'standing.'[19] And that, one might think, is significant, since whatever standing consists in, it seems that we do not have a right to blame only in virtue of having a normative power to set down standards with which others have a duty to comply. This suggests that Radzik has work to do to show that authority in rebuke is sufficiently similar to that involved in formal punishment.

7 WHAT DO WE NEED FROM OUR RESPONSES TO WRONGDOING?

As I mentioned earlier, the fascinating questions that Radzik's discussion raises can be fully addressed only by a taxonomy that sets out some of the

---

[18] On normative powers, see Joseph Raz, *Practical Reason and Norms* (Oxford: Oxford University Press, 1975); and David Owens, *Shaping the Normative Landscape* (Oxford: Oxford University Press, 2012).

[19] The debate over this can perhaps be traced back to Stephen Darwall, *The Second-Person Standpoint: Morality, Respect and Accountability* (Cambridge, MA: Harvard University Press, 2006). For a critical take, see Macalester Bell, "Standing to Blame: A Critique," in *Blame: Its Nature and Norms*, ed. Coates and Tognazzini, 263–81.

various ways in which we can respond to wrongdoing, categorized in ways we have reason to distinguish. In attempting now to give a brief explanation of this landscape, I would like to start by asking what kinds of needs we have that might bear on the character of our responses to wrongdoing. In the following, I tell a speculative, developmental story about these needs that takes its inspiration from Bernard Williams's appeal to functionalist, state of nature stories about needs for the concepts of truth and truthfulness.[20] However, as in Williams's own genealogical myth-making, the developmental nature of the story is not essential to it, and nothing I say here depends on the truth of any particular claim about the temporal order of the development of these concepts. Rather, what I attempt to do here is to show something about the logical structure or interrelations between various kinds of responses to wrongdoing and to show how distinctions that we operate with can be traced back to things that plausibly we do need from our conceptualization of such situations.

Perhaps the most basic kinds of needs for the development of concepts to do with responding to wrongdoing are *social control needs*. A social group needs to have broadly accepted ways of doing things – whether these are standards, rules, principles, values, and so on – and it needs to have ways of preventing or at least discouraging its members from violating those values. Education and socialization are important ways in which this is carried out. Socialization involves inculcation of members into a shared evaluative outlook – that is, particular values that members of the group take one another as having a responsibility to take seriously and respect in their actions. But it also involves making members to some extent receptive to peer pressure, and the inculcation of an attitude of caring about what others think about you. Such action can prevent people from violating the basic social rules in the first place. However, as well as prevention and discouragement, there are also social control needs that have to do with dealing with those who do violate the basic shared standards. There might be a need to subject those who violate those standards to various kinds of pressure to bring them back into line. Such pressure might range from physical harming or deprivation of liberty or movement to subjection to unpleasant outbursts of emotion, such as shouting, or emotional withdrawal, where an individual is made to feel isolated from the rest of the group. This is a way of bringing people back

---

[20] Bernard Williams, *Truth and Truthfulness: An Essay in Genealogy* (Princeton NJ: Princeton University Press, 2002). See also Miranda Fricker, "What's the Point of Blame? A Paradigm-Based Explanation," *Noûs* 50 (2016): 165–83.

into the fold when they are tempted to violate the values a general attachment to which is necessary for the survival and maintenance of the group. This sketch of social control needs deliberately relies on a rather simple conception of a social group, and a simplified conception of agents' capabilities and motivations. I suspect that social groups large and small have such mechanisms, and perhaps do need them. But they are not all that they need.

Because members of social groups are agents who are capable, to varying degrees, of reasoning and imagination and engagement with the realm of value, and because these features are important aspects of their identity, both in their self-conception and in the way they are seen in the group, social control needs can develop in ways that specifically exploit and also respect those cognitive abilities. Thus social control needs are very often *communicative needs*. By this I mean that, if we have social control needs for the alignment of attitudes among members of a social group, we will often meet those needs not simply by creating incentives for members to avoid divergent behavior but by appealing to agents' understanding, offering them reasons for doing certain things or refraining from certain things. Our reasons for taking this communicative route can be reasons of efficacy – sometimes a disposition to behave in certain ways is more robust when rooted in the agent's understanding. But the identity of the agent as a reasoning member of the community can also take on an importance in its own right, and so there can also be reasons of respect for employing communicative means rather than simply "tiger control."[21] Furthermore, there can be communicative needs in relation to wrongdoing that are not simply social control needs. These can be needs, for instance, that have to do with not just communicating with people in order to bring them back into line, but communicating with them because having the right kind of understanding, and leading the right kind of life, can be important in its own right. That is, it can be important not simply because it allows you to fit in with the social group of which you are part but also because it is important in its own right for a person, or a group, to exercise their intelligence and live the best way they can by their own lights. Thus it can be important in itself, and not simply for the purposes of increasing desirable social conformity, to criticize a person whose actions are unjustifiable.

However, human beings are not simply reasoning social animals; they are also creatures of emotion. They care about each other, and care about themselves, care that people get the treatment they ought to, and care that their importance is reflected in the actions and intentions of others. For this reason I suspect that we have *expressive needs* and that social practices such as those that revolve around wrongdoing will need to be constructed in such a way as to accommodate such needs. One simple type of expressive need might be a need to relieve emotional pressure, to let off steam, or to vent our feelings. On this simple view we might see expressions of emotion as consisting in actions like thumping the table in anger. Such action need appeal to no audience, and might be done just as well in private. Some reactions to wrongdoing can be like this, such as simple outbursts of frustration or rage (perhaps this fits Radzik's reaction to the repairman?). However, for some expressive actions, this simple picture is too simple. For instance, it can also be the case that expressive actions are deployed in order to serve our communicative needs. We might perform an expression of some emotion in order to show a person that we feel that emotion (or that it would be appropriate to feel it). I suspect that intentionally communicating information about our emotional states by engaging in certain expressive behavior requires that there is "natural" or nonintentional expressive behavior that is associated with an emotion and that is referenced by the agent who wants to communicate, say, that they are angry by thumping the table. This kind of communicative expression of emotion is suggested by some of what Radzik wants to say about responses to wrongdoing: for instance, when she says that in a rebuke you "send the message that *you* are angry with him."[22]

However, in addition to these two categories of expression of emotion, the venting and the communicative, I have argued in other work that there is a third category of expressive action. Expressive action in this sense involves performing an action because it is expressively powerful in relation to the way an emotion portrays a situation.[23] Take the case of the faithful kneeling in church out of reverence for the greatness of God, or a bereaved son helping to carry his father's coffin to the grave. It is not that these actions are "natural" expressions of the emotions concerned. Neither need it be the case that the agents are attempting to communicate to anyone about what they are feeling – it is not a form of reporting that is involved. Rather, the actions can be seen as attempts to do something that *symbolizes* or embodies the salient features of the

---

[22] Radzik, Chapter 1 in this volume, 13.
[23] See Bennett, "Expressive Actions"; and my "How and Why to Express the Emotions: Romantic and Post-Kantian Perspectives" (unpublished manuscript).

situation they take themselves to be in. What I mean by this is that these agents are involved in doing something that captures or does justice to the salient features of their situation as they see it and that they attempt to do justice to these situations by performing actions that reflect or symbolize their salient features. In virtue of this symbolic connection, the kneeling and the coffin-carrying certainly say something about the situation or have a meaning: they convey or embody an attitude. The kneeling, for instance, means the recognition of being in the presence of a being of incomparable worth; the coffin-carrying means losing and saying goodbye to someone deeply important to you, and wanting to take the last chance to take care of that person on their final journey. I suggest that, as well as communicative and venting needs, we have expressive needs of this sort as well. That is, we sometimes need to engage in behavior that attempts symbolically to do justice to our situation, as when we punch the air in delight, or ruffle a child's hair, or hug the clothes of an absent loved one.[24] We do this in order to lift certain events or situations out of the ongoing flow of one event after another, and to preserve or dwell on them. But when the symbolic actions are apt, we can also find them a satisfying vehicle through which to express our emotions. Some of the most powerful times when we reach for expressive actions of this sort are in 'rites of passage' moments involving birth, death, welcoming, and leaving, but also moments involving transgression. Thus if there is such a category of expressive actions, we would expect to find that there are some responses to wrongdoing that are part of our vocabulary because they are expressively powerful in relation to the situation of wrongdoing.

Finally, I would suggest that in addition to the needs already mentioned, we also have *normative needs*. That is, our imagined social group, the members of which desire predictable and reliable, secure social interaction, but who can also reason and engage with value, whose identity partly depends on their ability to reason and comply with the demands of value, and who have emotions and express them in various ways, needs also to develop deontic concepts such as duty, obligation, right, permission – and transgression as a violation of duty or obligation. One reason they need to develop the deontic is a social control reason – that a social group needs to have not only values to which to aspire but also enforceable

---

[24] These examples are drawn from Rosalind Hursthouse, "Arational Actions," *Journal of Philosophy* 88, no. 2 (1991): 57–68.

standards that members will attract criticism from their fellows for flouting. When a society holds to a common conception of enforceable standards, this allows there to be effective, devolved social control without any active central coordination. However, there can also be intrinsic reasons for deontic structures to emerge. For instance, once there is a conception of expressive action, the idea can emerge that there is an appropriate expressive response to the presence of creatures of value (just as there is an appropriate expressive response to God). The appropriate expressive response to humanity, if one is sympathetic to the Kantian view, is respect – not kneeling, but a kind of self-limiting and noninterference that expresses respect for rational agency's capacities for self-determination. Thus the idea that rational agents have a domain or sovereignty that is inviolate might emerge as an expressively compelling response to the dignity of rational agency. And an idea of duty or obligation can emerge that says that one must not approach or deal with these creatures in ways that fail to do justice to their value – that to do so is to violate that value. Thus the concept of duty and obligation can emerge from the concept of expressive action. And hence an idea of transgression can emerge as the idea of something that violates the expressive demands of the value in question.

Expressive needs and social control needs can therefore help to constitute our sense of obligation. They lead us to see certain actions as being such that we are required to perform or avoid them. However, once this is in place, it can also be the case that certain preventive, communicative, or expressive actions can themselves come to be seen as obligatory, including such actions that relate to wrongdoing. Thus members of this social group could come to see themselves as under an obligation not just to respect rational agents but also to engage in communicative or expressive actions that target wrongdoers who have violated obligations to respect rational agents. In other words, a conception of reactive action can emerge; such reactive actions, as we have seen, can be deterrent, or communicative, or venting, or symbolic; and we can come to see ourselves as under an obligation to perform the appropriate communicative or expressive action.

Some obligations are derived from social control needs; some are derived from attempts expressively to do justice to the nature of value; whereas some obligations are second-order or reactive in the sense that they govern reactions to the responses of others to those value- or need-based obligations. However, another category that can emerge once we have this conception of obligation in place and the conception of expressive action is that of ritual action. By this I mean the idea of an action that is expressively powerful in relation to some situation and through engagement in which one changes one's normative state, either losing certain obligations, or incurring obligations, or otherwise altering obligations, and so on. One example is the case of 'paying respects' – for instance, by kneeling before the monarch, symbolizing deference, one makes it permissible for oneself to address the monarch, where it would not otherwise have been permissible. Or by undertaking an exchange of rings, two marriage partners incur obligations to love and cherish each other, for richer and poorer, and so on. Or by undertaking penitential actions that symbolize her alienation from God, the sinner cleanses herself of her sins. These are examples in which some action that has to meet standards of expressive power or expressive adequacy in relation to the agent's situation are undertaken in such a way as to 'cleanse' an agent of obligations incurred by sin or to put them into a new normative state where new permissions or obligations apply to them. Normally, only certain people can undertake given ritual actions: either they need a certain kind of formal authority or they need to be in a relevant normative position, such as the penitent. Thus ritual action requires some kind of authority or standing. It can be that a community that has the concept of expressive action, and the concept of obligation, develops the idea that in regard to wrongdoing some ritual actions are necessary for those with the standing to perform them. For instance, it might be taken to be necessary to dissociate oneself from wrongful action, whether one's own or that of others, thereby avoiding complicity in that action, and disavowing acquiescence in it, by undertaking some kind of expressively adequate action that is established as the ritual form for bringing about such normative change. One might gain the standing to do so from having been involved in the wrongdoing in some way, such as being its perpetrator or victim, or being otherwise closely connected.

One last thing to add to this sketch of our conceptual map is that an increasingly individualistic version of our social group might take up this idea of ritual action and transform it into the idea of a normative domain of sovereignty that can be altered through normative power and voluntary obligation to allow the agents to bind themselves to others, to rule over others, to allow others into their domain when otherwise they would have been under an expressive obligation not to interfere. Voluntary obligations are those that can be created, waived, transferred, or otherwise altered at will, normally by a speech act that communicates the intention thereby to so alter those obligations. Powers to alter obligation voluntarily include practical authority, which we talked about earlier, as well as promise, gift, and consent.[25] Thus, if one possesses the power of practical authority, one may create obligations for others, and make them accountable to oneself for their compliance, and liable to enforcement of the obligation should they fail to comply. In promise one creates obligations for oneself; in consent one waives rights and thereby makes things permissible for another person in regard to one's domain. These powers, like the ritual action to which they are related, require that one who exercises them should have a certain authority or standing and act within their proper jurisdiction. The availability of these powers allows agents to create new normatively binding structures that allow for the creation of complex cooperative groups coordinated by a central authority, or long-term reciprocal cooperative arrangements. These arrangements are valuable not only because they increase human productive capacity in reliable ways but also because they are exercises of autonomy by which human beings author their own lives and shape the normative relations in which they are involved.[26]

The story that I have just told looks at various kinds of needs that relate to wrongdoing: I have argued that there are social control, communicative, expressive, and normative needs. Each of these needs can be viewed as distinct from the others, though of course, as I have suggested in the discussion, they can interact: for instance, with communicative strategies being used to meet social control needs, with expressions of emotion being used to communicate, or with expressive, symbolic actions being used to bring about normative changes. Now my aim in providing this sketch is not to explain why concepts of obligation, expressive action, ritual, or so on emerged in actual fact. Neither is it to justify our use of these concepts or to show why they are valid. As I said above, my aim is, rather, to suggest that, given that as social animals we have certain needs, and given the assumption of certain preexisting conceptual resources, we can see the rationale for our coming to have certain other concepts. And it is this range of concepts that I think is necessary better to understand the range of responses to wrongdoing that Radzik is dealing with in her discussion. In order to understand whether, for example, rebukes should be classified as punishments, we need to understand what else rebukes might be if they are

---

[25] See, e.g., Joseph Raz, "Voluntary Obligations and Normative Powers: Part II," *Proceedings of the Aristotelian Society* 46 (1972): 79–102.

[26] For this theme, see Joseph Raz, "Promises and Obligations," in *Law, Morality and Society: Essays in Honour of H. L. A. Hart*, ed. P. M. S. Hacker and Joseph Raz (Oxford: Clarendon Press. 1977), 210–28; Owens, *Shaping the Normative Landscape*; and my "Review of David Owens' *Shaping the Normative Landscape*," *Jurisprudence* 6 (2015): 364–70.

not punishments, and what reasons we might have for upholding certain classificatory schema. That is what I have been attempting to work toward in this section. Let us now turn to look at responses to wrongdoing in particular, and how the taxonomy of this section relates to the questions we raised about Radzik's account earlier.

8 HOW TO DO THINGS WITH BLAME AND SOCIAL PUNISHMENT

What I have provided in the previous section is an account of some of the things that might push a community of moral agents to develop certain ways of thinking about their responses to wrongdoing, and to draw distinctions among those responses that reflect important differences in the 'push' behind them. From the categories drawn up in my story, we can identify a whole range of possible responses to wrongdoing that do different things. They can:

a) do something unpleasant to someone as a deterrent aimed at social control;
b) aim at social control through the communication of moral criticism, by attempting to change someone's attitudes;
c) communicate moral criticism for the purpose of pursuing or affirming moral truth and changing a person's attitudes for the better for its own sake (because having truthful moral attitudes is inherently preferable);
d) communicate moral criticism while venting emotion;
e) communicate moral criticism while also reporting an occurrent emotional state;
f) communicate moral criticism while subjecting someone to unpleasant venting of emotion for the purposes of social control;
g) aim to do justice to the wrongdoing by performing an act with expressive power in relation to that wrongdoing;
h) aim to change one's own normative state in relation to the wrongdoing by ritual action, for instance, by dissociation, but where this requires that one have the appropriate ritual standing.

Furthermore, we saw that any of (a)–(h) can in principle be things that it is obligatory to do in the aftermath of wrongdoing. Whether they are or are not will depend on further normative theorizing (though some responses on the list, such as (d), might be unlikely candidates). And we might also add that further hybrids, such as a combination of (g) with (b), (c), or (e), might be possible – for instance, where an action that has expressive power is used in order to make the communication of moral criticism more vivid and effective.

With this taxonomy in mind, I now want to try to identify what Radzik takes a rebuke to be. She distinguishes rebuke from moral criticism and from overt blame, and I take it that these latter categories occupy something like (b) or (c). What distinguishes rebuke from moral criticism and overt blame is the expression of anger. Therefore, on this basis I would locate her idea of rebuke in (d), (e), or (f). However, we can now return to the question we raised earlier of whether the Hax examples of 'punishment' are rebukes. As I said earlier, one striking thing about these examples is that they tend to involve emotional withdrawal and disengagement *rather than* angry engagement with the wrongdoer. On my interpretation of these withdrawal cases, therefore, what is going on here is something more like (g) and (h). In other words, I understand withdrawal in these cases to be a 'fitting' response to wrongdoing because it is an expressively powerful symbol of the way in which the wrongdoer has 'broken' the terms of the relationship, violating some of the basic values and demands of membership in that relationship. In withdrawing, the agents need not be attempting to communicate anything; rather, they might simply find the action of withdrawal to be compelling because they feel that there is nothing more important that they can do in the situation except to disavow it, that is, to do justice to the magnitude of the wrong by an action that reflects how they experience that wrong, namely, as a breaking of good relations.

Furthermore, the taxonomy we have drawn up now allows me to be slightly more precise about my concern that the withdrawal cases are closer to punishment than are rebukes. For on my understanding, the concept of punishment is the concept of an expressive act, something falling into category (g) or (h). As I said earlier, punishment is an act in which the imposition of hard treatment *means* disapproval. As we can now put it, the imposition of hard treatment is an act that is supposed to be expressively powerful in relation to the situation of wrongdoing by virtue of its symbolically reflecting or capturing the salient features of that situation in the way that kneeling captures the attitude of deference or carrying the coffin captures the attitude of grief. The expressive actions, as we said earlier, stand for or embody the attitude. On my own view, it is not so much hard treatment that has this symbolic role as it is the deprivation of treatment that the person being punished would otherwise have a justified normative expectation of being able to enjoy. Deprivation is symbolically resonant in the way that withdrawal is: it captures something about the way that the wrongdoer is perceived as having broken normative community.[27] Furthermore, formal punishment is typically a case of (h), whereby a punishing authority disavows some action committed within its purview through ritualistic dissociation from the wrongdoer's action brought about by punishment.[28]

Now the crucial thing is not the verbal issue of which responses to wrongdoing we end up deciding to call 'punishment.' More important is recognizing how different kinds of responses fit in to one or other of the categories I have distinguished. Categorizing these responses in this way means that we understand the actions better – so we can understand better what is being done with each of these responses – but also what it might take to justify them.

9 CONCLUSION

In this response I have taken issue with the strategy that Radzik employs to argue for rebukes being informal social punishment. The problem with her strategy is that meeting the elements of the definition does not guarantee that rebukes are punishments; rather, we have to look at whether those elements are present in rebuke in the same way in which they are in punishment. Having noted this problem, I also raised some questions about whether rebukes do involve expressing disapproval, harming, or claiming authority, in the same way as punishment does. In order to resolve these questions, however, we need more than simply a conceptual analysis of punishment or a description of our use of that term. We need an explanation of the range of different responses that we might have developed, or might have reason to develop, and then to locate rebukes and punishments within that range. As it seems to me, setting out the range of different responses allows us to see that there are important differences between rebukes and punishments. Punishment is particularly problematic to justify, not just because it involves intentionally harming (many of the other responses do so as well) but because it is committed to the idea that by refusing to engage in normal relations with the wrongdoer one has the normative power thereby to dissociate oneself from what that wrongdoer did, and hence to avoid acquiescence and complicity in their action.

[27] See, e.g., my "The Expressive Function of Blame," in *Blame: Its Nature and Norms*, ed. Coates and Tognazzini, 66–83.

[28] See my "Penal Disenfranchisement," *Criminal Law and Philosophy* 10 (2016): 411–25; and "How Should We Argue for a Censure Theory of Punishment?," in *Penal Censure: Engagements within and beyond Desert Theory*, ed. Antje du Bois-Pedain and Anthony E. Bottoms (Oxford: Hart, 2019), 67–84.

CHAPTER 5

On Social Punishment

George Sher

To those of us who are not criminals, the good opinion of others looms far larger than any criminal sanction. I may fret about whether to have a third or fourth beer at a party if I will be driving, but I rarely spend much time thinking about passing counterfeit money, smuggling drugs, beating others up, or sodomizing them against their will. Maybe I would consider doing some of these things if the penalties were not attached, but they are and so I do not. By contrast, although the price of social disapproval is far less serious, an awareness of its possibility is never far below the surface. We regularly calculate social costs when we consider telling off-color jokes, disclosing unpopular opinions, wearing yesterday's clothes, or wedging references to our own accomplishments into conversations on other topics. When we guess wrong, we pay a price – often a heavy one – of embarrassment and shame. What others think of us matters a lot.

And that gives others a lot of power *over* us. Because we take the reactions of our fellows seriously, they are often able to shape our behavior by reacting positively when we conform to the norms they favor and negatively when we do not (and we, of course, can return the favor). Like any other form of power, this one can be used either well or badly, so we are in need of principles to guide its use. The questions of what these principles might look like, and how they might be justified, have received strikingly little philosophical attention – far less attention, certainly, than the corresponding questions about the principles that ought to govern the state's use of coercive force. But with Linda Radzik's series of lectures, that is about to change; for her aim is precisely to sketch a theory of what she calls "social punishment." It is an original and exciting project, and we are in her debt for undertaking it.

In its broadest form, the question that I see as motivating her inquiry is when and why we should deploy the various mechanisms of informal censure in response to failures to conform to social norms. But that is not quite how Radzik herself defines the project, and it will be helpful to begin by noting the differences. Two in particular stand out. First, although many of the norms whose violation elicits the strongest forms of social disapproval have no particular moral content – think, for example, of norms of propriety, decency, decorum, familiarity and distance, and personal hygiene – the ones on which Radzik focuses are exclusively moral. And, second, although the mechanisms through which social pressure works are largely psychological, Radzik's central example in Chapter 2 is a boycott of a corporate entity that lacks the kind of psychology on which these mechanisms work. A coffee company is incapable of craving human contact, introjecting the disapproval of others, or having either high or low self-esteem.

Of these two features of her account, the second may simply reflect a desire to accommodate a culturally salient set of examples, but the first has real philosophical bite. As we will see, Radzik's justification of social punishment relies heavily on the moral nature of the violated norms, and would not work without it. This raises interesting questions about what she could or should say about using something analogous to social punishment to reinforce important *non*moral norms. However, because my topic is her own theory, I will not address these questions but instead will move directly to what she says.

Radzik's strategy in developing her theory is to take what has been said about legal punishment as her guide and to ask which aspects of it do and do not carry over to the informal interpersonal context. She argues that there is enough continuity to warrant an extension of the term 'punishment' because both contexts provide opportunities for the authorized, intentional, reprobative, reactive infliction of harm. She argues, as well, that in the social no less than the legal context, the most appealing justification of punishment combines forward- and backward-looking elements. Like legal punishment, social punishment is justified only if it is both deserved and expected to produce good consequences. It is only when she gets to the content of the requisite forward- and backward-looking elements that Radzik's treatment becomes nonstandard.

For, first, unlike most others who maintain that punishment requires a form of desert, Radzik balks at the idea that harm or suffering can be good. That idea, she suggests, is "bloodthirsty," and to avoid having to accept it, she argues, first, that what is deserved is coercion rather than harm and, second, that wrongdoers deserve this treatment only in the sense that they have forfeited their usual right not to be subjected to it. Although the second of these moves is familiar, the first represents a significant departure from other retributivist accounts.

Like other forfeiture theorists, Radzik needs to invoke the good consequences of punishing in order to bridge the gap between the claim that
wrongdoers have forfeited their right not to be punished and the claim that
punishment is actually called for. However, unlike most others who take
this line, she focuses less on the familiar benefits of deterrence and
incapacitation than on certain other advantages that social punishment
offers. These benefits are said to accrue to the victims of wrongdoing, to
society, and to the wrongdoer himself: the victim benefits through a
reaffirmation of his worth and social standing, society by repair of ruptured
relationships, and the wrongdoer himself by the opportunity to improve
and make amends. This reconstruction of the benefits of social punishment is Radzik's second main departure from the familiar literature on
punishment.

This, clearly, is an interesting and novel theory about a neglected area of
our social lives, and my aim in what follows is to look more closely at its
details. To do so, I will comment first on the theory's retributive component and then on what Radzik says about the benefits of social
punishment.

I

Why, first, does she take the justification of social punishment to require a
retributive element at all? Her answer – the standard one – is that if its
justification turned entirely on the benefits of punishing, then we could
sometimes be justified in punishing the innocent instead of, or in addition
to, the guilty. To avoid this implication, we must take punishment to
require guilt as well as good consequences; and to understand what guilt
adds, we must explain how it alters the normative situation. Like many
others who take the justification of punishment to involve a retributive
element, Radzik uses the concept of desert as a kind of shorthand for
whatever it is about the wrongdoer's guilt that provides this explanation.
However, unlike these others, she is deeply suspicious of the central
thought that unites most retributive theories.

For whatever their differences, most retributivists agree that there is
something about previous wrongdoing that reverses the usual moral status
of what a person does not want or finds unpleasant – or, in a word, his
suffering. On some accounts, what has changed is what we might call the
valence of the suffering: on its own, it is bad or disvaluable, but if the
suffering party has previously transgressed, then it is good or valuable. On
other accounts the change is deontic: inflicting suffering is normally

wrong, but inflicting it as punishment can be right. However, against the first of these claims, Radzik writes that it

is a repugnant, bloodthirsty view because it counts the suffering of other human beings as intrinsically desirable. The pure retributivist might emphasize that she only values the suffering of the guilty, but I hardly see how this helps. The suffering of the wrongdoer is portrayed as a good in itself, which justifies punishment even if it makes neither the victim, nor the wrongdoer, nor anyone else better off.[1]

And although she does not explicitly say so, I strongly suspect that she would have analogous objections to the claim that a person's past wrongdoing can make it right to make him suffer now.

Because she has these objections, Radzik confronts a difficult task. On the one hand, she must explain how past wrongdoing can play a role in justifying social sanctions, but on the other, she must do so without endorsing the suffering that those sanctions inflict. In an effort to discharge this task, she considers and rejects a number of proposals, among them the suggestions that what the wrongdoer deserves is not suffering but only (1) a negative judgment of what he has done, (2) an expression of disapproval of his transgression, (3) a communicative act designed to inform him of his shortcomings, (4) the reactive attitude of resentment, or (5) an attempt to persuade him that he should not have acted as he did. In each case, she rejects the proposal on the grounds that it does not sufficiently acknowledge the connection between punishment and genuine hard treatment. In my view, this part of her discussion is exactly right, and I have nothing critical to say about it. I am, however, less convinced by the positive proposal that she advances in their place.

As I noted above, the two main elements of Radzik's backward-looking view are, first, that what is deserved as social punishment is (a kind of) coercion rather than suffering and, second, that the claim that wrongdoers deserve to be coerced implies not that they *must* be pressured to change their ways but only that they have forfeited their right not to be. Of these moves, the substitution of coercion for suffering partially defuses the charge of bloodthirstiness by introducing a less raw form of hard treatment, while the substitution of permission to coerce for the necessity of doing so further defuses it by relegating what is nasty about punishment to a secondary, instrumental role. Thus, taken together, the two moves represent Radzik's solution to the problem she has set for herself.

---

[1] Linda Radzik, Chapter 2 in this volume, 26.

Does this solution work? One question that it raises is whether both of its elements are really necessary. If we want to avoid endorsing the infliction of suffering in any form, can't we do so by simply equating the relevant form of hard treatment with coercion rather than suffering? And if we want to avoid endorsing hard treatment for its own sake, can't we do so by simply insisting that this is never justified except when done for some good purpose? Because the two aims seem separable, there is an obvious question about how they are related. However, as a deep-dyed retributivist, I have a hard time getting my mind around either aim, and neither do I have a good grip on the conception of bloodthirstiness that is somehow supposed to unite them. Thus, instead of pursuing any of this further, I will simply accept both aims and will confine my attention to Radzik's strategies for realizing them.

Let's begin with the proposal that the hard treatment that is justified when it is administered as social punishment is coercion rather than suffering. Because it is *social* punishment that we are dealing with, what Radzik means by "coercion" cannot be either physical forcing or threats of physical harm. Instead, what she has in mind is the loss of a certain kind of liberty – namely, being free from having our emotions manipulated and our choice options narrowed. This conception of coercion meshes nicely with the forfeiture aspect of her account, in that she maintains that people generally have a right not to be coerced in these ways, but that they forfeit this right when they act wrongly. This connection emerges clearly when she writes that

according to the view I am defending here – that the object of desert in cases of wrongdoing is a limitation of liberty – the harm does appear to touch on a right. Arguably, people generally have a moral right not to be subjected to the intentional manipulation of their emotions and their choice options, even when the manipulation in question is carried out simply through speech or social avoidance.[2]

It is, thus, by substituting the harm of being coerced for that of being made to suffer that Radzik attempts to thread the needle between being unacceptably bloodthirsty and being too wimpy to countenance any form of hard treatment.

But there are problems here, the most obvious of which is that the right in question is one that few theorists have acknowledged, and one that seems highly dubious on its merits. Do I really have a right not to be

---

[2] Ibid., 38.

subjected to the intentional manipulation of my emotions? If I do, isn't it violated daily by advertisers, political candidates, panhandlers, charity mailers, and everyone who uses rhetoric instead of reason to get me to believe something? And are my rights really also violated whenever someone else intentionally manipulates my choice options? Am I wronged when the supermarket intentionally limits my options to not getting English muffins and paying $2.49 for them? Does my wife violate my rights when she makes it clear that she won't watch the ball game with me unless I watch *Better Call Saul* with her? Does my friend do me dirty when she tells me that she won't be able read my manuscript until next week?

As these questions suggest, Radzik's formulation of the right that she takes us to forfeit by acting wrongly is at a minimum incomplete. To move it in the direction of plausibility, she must somehow distinguish the acceptable ways of manipulating people's emotions and shaping their option sets from the unacceptable ones. I am very skeptical about her ability to accomplish the first part of this task because emotional appeals are such an important part of the ways in which we relate to each other. Every human being on earth has areas of vulnerability and need, and everyone is sometimes demanding, sometimes hopeful, sometimes disappointed, and sometimes irascible. A social world in which people standardly attempted to conceal these reactions out of respect for their fellows' rights not to be manipulated would not be a world that any of us would recognize.

The second part of the task – to distinguish acceptable from unacceptable ways of limiting people's option sets – may at first glance appear more tractable because both philosophy and the law have had a lot to say about this. However, when one person tries to get another to do something by proposing to withhold a benefit or impose a harm if the other does not do it, the standard way of showing that his proposal is illegitimate is precisely to argue that he has no right to do what he is proposing. The thief has no right to shoot you if you withhold your money because you have a right to keep your money without being shot. But this kind of rejoinder is useless in the current context because the question at issue is precisely whether people *do* have a general right to go about their business without being avoided or shunned or chastised or disapproved of. Radzik's view, if I have understood it, is that people do have such a general right and that it is precisely this right that they forfeit when they act wrongly. However, if that is her view, then she is hardly in a position to defend it by insisting that no one has the right to deprive anyone of the option of acting as he pleases without being avoided, shunned, chastised, or disapproved of; for to say this would simply be to beg the question in favor of the right that is under discussion. It is of course possible that she might be able to defend that right in some other way, but I cannot imagine what that way might be.

There is, moreover, a further and even more serious difficulty with Radzik's attempt to avoid endorsing the infliction of suffering by identifying the relevant form of hard treatment exclusively with a certain kind of coercion: namely, that coercion of this kind works precisely because it *does* involve the infliction of (a minor form of) suffering. To bring this out, we need only ask ourselves why anyone should *care* about not being embarrassed, shamed, reprimanded, called out, censured, or shunned. The obvious answer, and the one on which Radzik's position depends, is that we want to avoid these forms of treatment because we find them *unpleasant*. It's no fun to be avoided, censured, or lectured at; neither is it fun to know that others feel let down or disappointed by what we have done. It is precisely the unpleasantness of these modes of treatment that makes it possible to motivate good behavior by removing the option of acting badly without being subject to them. Moreover, as far as I can see, there is no real difference between making things unpleasant for a person and inflicting a modicum of suffering on him. And for this reason, I cannot see that Radzik's substitution of coercion for suffering opens up any daylight at all between her and the other retributivists whose attitude toward suffering she deplores.

To bring this out, we need only remind ourselves that the strategy of understanding hard treatment in terms of coercion rather than suffering is available not only to kinder, gentler social punishers like Radzik, but also to the more bloody-minded members of the retributivist tribe. Consider, for example, the proponent of the lex talionis who takes justice to require an eye for an eye, and who therefore maintains those who torture others must now be tortured in their turn. A retributivist of this stripe will presumably argue that there is a general right not to be tortured and that it is precisely the torturer's violation of this right that now dictates the torture that he has coming. Thus, the lex talionis retributivist can recast what is significant about his torturing of the torturer as the fact that it coercively deprives him of the option of being an untortured torturer. By Radzik's reckoning, this should allow the lex talionis retributivist to sidestep the charge of bloodthirstiness by insisting that the form of hard treatment that he takes the torturer to deserve is not the suffering of having his fingernails torn out, but only the blander harm of being coercively deprived of the liberty of torturing others *without* having his fingernails torn out. But that would not be a convincing rejoinder.

There is, I think, no escaping the connection between the administration of deserved punishment and the infliction of suffering. There may be isolated instances in which getting the punishment one deserves is not unpleasant, as when a rich inside trader has so much money that the fine does not matter to him or a traffic offender does not mind losing his license for thirty days because he has no immediate need to drive. However, if these forms of punishment were not things that people generally find unpleasant or painful, then they would not be forms of punishment at all. I have actually seen it proposed – I can't remember where – that we might be able to prevent more crimes by paying certain classes of would-be criminals not to offend than we now do by following through on our threats to incarcerate them when they do offend. This idea seems crazy because of the perverse incentives that any such scheme would create; but even if this problem could be overcome, the payments would not count as punishment because the mechanism through which they produced their good effects would not operate through a desire to avoid some form of unpleasantness.

2

The lesson I draw from these considerations is that any retributivist, Radzik included, must assign some kind of positive role to the suffering of the person who is punished. At least to this extent, you cannot be a retributivist without getting your hands dirty. But even if Radzik cannot fully avoid the charge of bloodthirstiness by understanding the relevant form of hard treatment as coercion or the limiting of options rather than suffering, she may still be able to minimize its force by downplaying the role of suffering in her overall justification. To do this, she need only invoke the consequentialist element of her justification to argue that on her account, unlike that of the purer retributivist, the infliction of suffering is valued not for its own sake but only as a means of bringing about good consequences in a non-rights-violating way.

In its generic form, this rejoinder is available to the proponents of all mixed theories of punishment. It works both for those who locate the good consequences of punishment exclusively in its deterrent effects and for those like Radzik who take a wider view. As I mentioned earlier, Radzik takes the benefits of social punishment to include not only deterrence but also the reinforcement of social norms, the reaffirmation of the victim's moral standing, the avoidance of complicity in wrongdoing, the reparation of whatever relationships the wrongdoer has ruptured, and the moral improvement of the wrongdoer himself. However, as she herself notes, to ground the generic version of the rejoinder in any of these good effects except the last is to expose oneself to the further objection that "there is still something offensive in using the wrongdoer as a mere means to securing these benefits to others."[3] Even if the wrongdoer has forfeited his right not to be coerced, or not to be made to suffer, the infliction of the coercion or suffering may still seem objectionable if its sole rationale is to benefit others.

Because she takes this objection seriously, Radzik insists that "any interference with the wrongdoer should be designed with an eye to the wrongdoer's good as well as the good of the victim and the community."[4] She argues, moreover, that the crucial benefit must be a moral one: "we should design our interference so as to support her abilities as a moral agent and to help her reclaim her place as a trusted member of the moral community."[5] Drawing on her excellent previous book *Making Amends*,[6] Radzik argues that these are precisely the consequences that ensue when agents acknowledge and take responsibility for their past transgressions. Thus, the view that she settles on is that "the proper goal of informally socially punishing a wrongdoer – the aim we should have when interfering with her liberty – is to morally pressure her to make amends for her own misdeed."[7]

Here again, I find it hard to get my mind around the worry that even if coercing someone or making him suffer violates none of his rights, it remains objectionable if it is done solely to benefit others. Especially as it applies to the coercive narrowing of another's options, this worry seems inconsistent with a vast range of legitimate self-protective and other-regarding actions. However, here again, too, I want to set this objection aside in order to concentrate on the specifics of Radzik's proposal. Granting the legitimacy of her assumption that the coercion must benefit the wrongdoer (and granting also her further assumption that the benefit must consist of his moral improvement), is she really warranted in concluding that the central justifying aim of social punishment is to induce the wrongdoer to make amends?

There are, I think, at least two gaps in the argument that she must fill. First, to link social punishment to the making of amends, she must

---

[3] Ibid., 41.
[4] Ibid.
[5] Radzik, Ch. 2, in this volume, 41.
[6] Linda Radzik, *Making Amends: Atonement in Morality, Law, and Politics* (New York: Oxford University Press, 2009).
[7] Ibid.

establish that moral pressure standardly or typically *leads* wrongdoers to make amends; and, second, to link the making of amends to moral improvement, she must establish that those who make amends always or usually become morally better as a result. Although each claim has a strong normative component, each is, in the end, a claim about how the world works. Thus, the obvious way to test the claims is to operationalize each with an eye to asking whether it is borne out by the empirical evidence. However, Radzik's discussion contains little along those lines, and I have neither the patience nor the expertise to go for the requisite slog through the social scientific literature (much less to construct the empirical tests myself). Thus, in what follows, I will simply call attention to some familiar considerations that appear to cast doubt on each claim.

Let's begin with the relation between making amends and becoming morally better. Summarizing the results of her earlier book, Radzik writes that "the making of amends typically requires three things from the wrongdoer: moral improvement, respectful communication, and the reparation of harm."[8] She writes as well that "moral improvement requires ceasing the wrongful action and committing oneself not to repeat it."[9] This seems right as far as it goes – a wrongdoer can hardly be said to make amends without resolving to do better in the future – but it leaves open the question of whether making such a resolution is sufficient for moral improvement or whether it is merely necessary. If simply resolving to improve is sufficient, then the resolution's continued efficacy in shaping future conduct will not be relevant. On this account, a wrongdoer who resolves to do better will count as morally improved even if he is a perpetual backslider whose resolution will have no lasting effect. By contrast, if making a sincere resolution to do better is only a *necessary* condition for making amends, then it will be plausible to add, as a further necessary condition, the requirement that the resolution stick. On this account, moral improvement will be a lasting (though not necessarily a permanent) condition of an agent. This, clearly, is the more plausible way of understanding the notion.

But adopting this interpretation also has its costs; for to show that social pressure can bring this form of moral improvement, we must look beyond its proximal effects. We must look beyond the resulting resolutions to do better because just as our resolutions to lose weight and exercise more are often swamped by entrenched habits and enduring temptations, so too are

---

[8] Ibid., 42.
[9] Ibid.

our resolutions to listen more carefully to others, bite back our surges of anger, and resist our selfish urges. If a form of social coercion is unpleasant enough, there will indeed be pressure to adopt whatever resolution will make it stop; but if the temptation to backslide is also strong, then there will also be pressure to violate the resolution later on. Which pressure wins out will no doubt depend on many factors: on the one hand, the agent's fear of renewed coercion and his desire to obey his own self-imposed laws, on the other the strength of the temptation to backslide and the amount of willpower that he can muster against it. Nevertheless, when the responses to social coercion are considered in the aggregate, the ones that involve lasting behavioral change are bound to represent only a fraction of the total. This raises questions both about how large that fraction is in fact likely to be and about how large it would have to be in order to support Radzik's claim that moral improvement is the general justifying aim of social punishment.

The second of these questions is again one that is raised by all mixed theories of punishment (as well as by all purely consequentialist theories). There must be some levels of deterrence that are too low to warrant the punishment schedules that produce them: the level will, for example, presumably be inadequate if a society punishes shoplifters either by cutting off their hands or by fining them trivial amounts. Thus, anyone who takes punishment to be justified by its ability to deter further crimes will owe us an account of which levels of deterrence are required to justify which forms of punishment; and analogous questions will be raised by all other consequentialist justifications, Radzik's included. But these questions have been much discussed in the punishment literature – see, for example, Bentham's classic treatment in his *Principles of Morals and Legislation*[10] – and this is not the place to advance them further. Thus, setting these issues to one side, I will proceed directly to the question of how much enduring moral improvement we can in fact expect social punishment to produce.

That depends, I think, on how expansive a notion of lasting improvement we have in mind. If we understand moral improvement in purely behavioral terms – if what matters is simply how often or seldom a wrongdoer reoffends – then we may expect the rate of improvement to track the harshness of the penalties that engender it. Roughly speaking, the harsher the penalties, the more the offender will fear their reapplication, and so the greater the likelihood that he will avoid doing what would

---

[10] Jeremy Bentham, *The Principles of Morals and Legislation* (Buffalo, NY: Prometheus Books, 1988), chs. 13–15.

trigger it. However, to understand moral improvement in this way would simply be to equate levels of moral improvement with levels of deterrence, and that is clearly not what Radzik has in mind. Against this, she writes that "atonement requires sincere changes in beliefs and attitudes and not just in behavior."[11] Thus, to clarify the relation between social punishment and moral improvement, we will need to gain a better understanding of the mechanisms through which social pressure can secure changes in belief and attitude.

Although the issues here are complicated, the general gist of Radzik's view is clear enough. As she sees it, the mechanism through which social punishment changes attitudes is partly rational and partly nonrational. The rational element is supplied by its communicative dimension: a well-designed punishment "will draw the wrongdoer's attention to the costs of his transgression, including negative reactive attitudes, and the weakening of trust and goodwill among his fellows."[12] But instead of relying exclusively on reason, social punishment also provides a nonrational motive for a change in attitude: "if the coercive aspects of punishment are well designed, they create incentives for the wrongdoer to reform his attitudes and behaviors."[13] Although the virtuous punisher "should hope that the communicative aspects of punishment will predominate over the coercive aspects," his reliance on each is both legitimate and necessary.[14]

There is, in general, nothing problematic about having more than one motive for performing a single action. We obviously find it easier to avoid doing what we recognize as wrong when we also expect our virtuous behavior to redound to our advantage. But things become more complicated when an agent is *not* aware that what he is doing is wrong, and when the task of social punishment is therefore both to instill the moral awareness that will move him to avoid such actions in the future and to provide him with additional motivation of the crasser, self-protective variety. Put most simply, the problem in such cases is that the educative and motivational functions of the punishment seem likely to work at cross-purposes.

For when someone threatens to make things unpleasant for us if we do not do as he says, our natural first reaction is not to align our will with his, but rather to view his demand as an unwelcome imposition. When we bow to a coercive threat, we do so not because we want to but because we have

---

[11] Radzik, Chapter 2 in this volume, 43.
[12] Ibid.
[13] Ibid.
[14] Ibid., 44.

to, and our resistance tends to make us unreceptive to whatever reasons might justify the coercion. Even if the coercer has a strong case, his strong-arm tactics will work against our willingness to consider it. The point I am making here goes beyond Locke's claim that "such is the nature of the understanding that it cannot be compelled to the belief of anything by outward force";[15] it is, in addition, that being forced to act on beliefs that we do not hold is actually likely to *repress* our receptiveness to them. Threats, though often effective at eliciting desired forms of behavior, are often ineffective at instilling the beliefs and attitudes that in fact justify the behavior. And, for this reason, what Radzik represents as the educative function of social punishment must often be at odds with what she represents as its motivating function.

This isn't a knock-down argument against her dual-use theory. For one thing, even if no one likes being pushed around, some are bound to resent it more than others, and those who resent it less may also be less resistant to attitudinal change. In addition, and more importantly, even if someone who alters his behavior in response to a threat is thereby rendered too resentful to alter his beliefs and attitudes right away, the longer-range effects of his altered behavior may themselves eventually put him in a position to do just that. As I argued at length in my book *Beyond Neutrality*,[16] a person who is bribed or threatened to do something whose value he does not appreciate – to take a required philosophy course, for example, or to live a drug-free life – may over time come to recognize the activity's value "from the inside." This is easiest to see when the value that is eventually recognized is hedonic or prudential – when the philosophy course turns out to be fun or abstention from drugs allows one to hold a decent job – but it also seems possible when the relevant form of value is less personal. An agent may initially avoid a certain form of wrongdoing only because he fears the ensuing social punishment, but may eventually come to recognize the moral reasons for avoiding it in the very course of doing so. If Radzik can establish a systematic link of this kind between the motivational and the educative effects of social punishment, then she will indeed be able to avoid the objection that the two effects are at cross-purposes.

[15] John Locke, "A Letter Concerning Toleration," in *John Locke on Politics and Education* (Roslyn, NY: Walter J. Black, 1947), 26.
[16] George Sher, *Beyond Neutrality: Perfectionism and Politics* (Cambridge: Cambridge University Press, 1997), ch. 3.

3

This concludes my discussion of the justification of social punishment that Radzik has offered. Although I have focused mainly on the aspects of her theory that I take either to require further elaboration or to invite some sort of objection, and although I have made it clear that I do not share some of the key assumptions on which the theory rests, I regard both the questions that she has raised and the answers she has provided as extremely important. It is impossible to work through her account without coming to recognize that she has located a set of phenomena that are absolutely central to our lived experience but that have received very little attention from analytic moral philosophers. The unresolved questions about her account are just what one would expect from an early exploration of an important new field of inquiry, and I am very much looking forward to seeing how they play themselves out.

CHAPTER 6

Punishment and Protest

Glen Pettigrove

I THE COMEDIAN

On Tuesday, December 4, 2018, the comedian Kevin Hart announced that he had accepted an invitation from the Academy of Motion Picture Arts and Sciences to host the televised broadcast of the 2019 Oscar Awards ceremony. While many applauded the Academy's choice, not everyone was happy. The writer Benjamin Lee responded to the announcement by tweeting, "And the Oscar for most homophobic host ever goes to ..." followed by a quote from a stand-up routine Hart had performed a number of times – including in his film *Seriously Funny* (2010) – in which he says, "One of my biggest fears is my son growing up and being gay."[1] In a follow-up tweet, Lee posted screenshots from Hart's Twitter account that featured gay slurs, along with the caption, "I wonder when Kevin Hart is gonna start deleting all his old tweets."[2] And that day *The Guardian* published an op-ed by Lee documenting Hart's use of homophobic language, his role in homophobic movies like *Get Hard* and *The Wedding Ringer*, and his refusal to apologize for homophobic jokes over the years.[3]

Lee was not alone in objecting to Hart's behavior. Awards Watch founder Erik Anderson tweeted, "Considering how many of the Oscars' biggest fans are women and gay men it's quite something for the Academy to hire a guy who beat one wife, cheated on another when she was eight months pregnant and said one of his biggest fears is his son growing up and

---

[1] Benjamin Lee@benfraserlee, *Twitter*, Dec. 4, 2018, https://twitter.com/benfraserlee/status/1070134637605867520?lang=en. The relevant portion of Seriously Funny can be seen here: www.youtube.com/watch?v=dd2M6WyQ9Bk (accessed Feb. 20, 2019).
[2] Benjamin Lee@benfraserlee, *Twitter*, Dec. 5, 2018, https://twitter.com/benfraserlee/status/1070413541012893696?lang=en (accessed Feb. 20, 2019).
[3] Benjamin Lee, "Oscar Host Kevin Hart's Homophobia Is No Laughing Matter," *The Guardian*, online edition, Dec. 5, 2018.

being gay."[4] Comedian Billy Eichner tweeted, "Many of us have jokes/ tweets we regret. I'm ok with tasteless jokes, depending on context. What bothers me about these is you can tell it's not just a joke – there's real truth, anger & fear behind these."[5] Zack Sharf and Michael Blackmon published articles on IndieWire and BuzzFeed expressing similar concerns.[6] And hundreds of people reposted Lee's, Anderson's, Eichner's, Sharf's, and Blackmon's remarks on various social media sites, adding their own comments to the groundswell of criticism. For example, Lee's original tweet was shared more than 400 times and liked by more than 1,000 readers. And the post that included images of Hart's old tweets was retweeted more than 900 times and liked by more than 2,000 people.

The Academy tried to defuse the situation by approaching Hart and telling him that if he wished to host the Oscars, he would need to apologize for his past remarks. In response, Hart posted a video on Instagram in which he offered excuses – e.g., those remarks are old, I'm not the same man I was when I made them, and I have already apologized for them – and refused to apologize. Rather than acknowledging the hurt he might have caused others, he dismissed those who objected to his behavior as "internet trolls" and "haters" who were out to destroy him.[7] And he found himself out of a job.

The Kevin Hart case is an example of what has become a remarkably familiar type. An individual behaves badly. Someone else – the recipient of the treatment, a friend, or a bystander – calls them out in a newspaper article, a blog post, a tweet, a Facebook status, or a YouTube video. A number of those who read the post or watch the video repost it with additional criticism. And both the original post and subsequent repostings attract comments from a still wider audience that is eager to add its voice to the chorus of those condemning the misdeed and its perpetrator.

Linda Radzik's insightful discussion of informal social punishment offers us a way to interpret occurrences of this type. She sees them as cases of punishment, albeit a punishment administered by one's peers using informal means. I will offer an alternative way to read them, namely, as

[4] Erik Anderson@awards_watch, *Twitter*, Dec. 5, 2018, https://twitter.com/awards_watch/status/ 1070144276447653888 (accessed Feb. 28, 2019).
[5] Billie Eichner@billyeichner, *Twitter*, Dec. 6, 2018, https://twitter.com/billyeickner/status/ 1070750816649207809 (accessed Feb. 28, 2019).
[6] Zack Sharf, "Kevin Hart Called Out for Homophobic Jokes after Being Named 2019 Oscars Host," *Indie Wire*, Dec. 5, 2018; and Michael Blackmon, "Kevin Hart Is Deleting Old Anti-Gay Tweets after Being Announced as Oscars Host," *BuzzFeed*, Dec. 6, 2018.
[7] kevinhart4real, Instagram, Dec. 7, 2018, www.instagram.com/p/BrEjHFCFe83/?utm_source=ig_ embed&utm_medium=loading (accessed Feb. 28, 2019).

protest. Since the norms for protest differ from those for punishment, the fact that many situations can be read as both protest and punishment poses a challenge for Radzik's attempt to use the category of informal social punishment to determine whether a particular course of action is permissible. In Section 2, I provide a brief summary of Radzik's account of social punishment and show how it helps us make sense of the Kevin Hart case. Section 3 describes a case that in many ways resembles Hart's, namely, that of William Sitwell. But whereas the actions in the Hart case appear to be an example of justified informal social punishment, Section 4 argues that those in the Sitwell case do not. Section 5 introduces an alternative concept, namely, protest, and suggests that protesting is governed by different norms than punishing. The final section shows that the Hart and Sitwell cases can also be read as instances of justified protest. This raises questions both about how we should choose between competing readings of a case and about the link between justified protest/punishment and justified action.

2 JUSTIFIED SOCIAL PUNISHMENT

In line with standard views, Radzik takes punishment to have five distinguishing features.[8] First, it *harms* the one on whom it is inflicted. The harm need not be an all-things-considered harm. For example, someone may ultimately benefit from being punished because it teaches him a lesson. Nevertheless, at the time it is administered, punishment must be something its recipient would prefer to forgo. Second, for the harm to be punishment, it must be *intentionally* inflicted. Injuries that are caused inadvertently can be every bit as painful, but if they are not inflicted knowingly and with the purpose of punishing, they are not punitive. Third, the harm must also be *reactive*. That is to say, it must be a response to the other party's failure to fulfill an obligation. Fourth, punitive actions are *reprobative*. Part of their aim is to "express disapproval of the one being punished."[9] Fifth, the person administering the harm must be *authorized* to do so. If they are not, their action is at best a form of vigilantism. Finally, what sets informal social punishment apart from punishment of other kinds is that it takes place between "social equals" rather than between a superior and a subordinate.[10]

---

[8] Linda Radzik, Chapter 1 in this volume, 9–11.
[9] Ibid., 10.
[10] Ibid., 11–12.

Returning to the Kevin Hart example, it looks like a clear instance of what Radzik is discussing. Kevin Hart was harmed by the criticism leveled against him. He suffered the pain of widespread, public shaming. He also lost his place on the biggest stage in the business and the prestige, publicity, and income that went with it. The harm was caused intentionally by (at least some of) those who criticized his behaviors. Admittedly, the overarching aim of the members of the Academy who decided Hart needed to apologize or forgo hosting the event was probably not to punish him. It was to avoid backlash from participants and prospective viewers who object to discrimination aimed at members of the LGBTQ+ community and from organizations like the Gay & Lesbian Alliance Against Defamation who campaign on their behalf. However, the intentionally chosen means to that end was to subject Hart to treatment he would rather have avoided. So it, too, would seem to fall under the heading of 'intentionally harming' broadly construed. The harmful actions were intended to express disapproval of Hart and his failure to respect those whose sexual orientation differs from his own. Moreover, insofar as all members of the moral community have the standing to criticize actions that harm or disrespect innocent others and the Academy has the right to decide whom it will employ, the public and the Academy were authorized to act as they did. Finally, the harm Hart suffered on Instagram, Twitter, Facebook, and the like was caused by social equals. It looks like a textbook case of informal social punishment.

Meeting the abovementioned conditions does not yet guarantee the punishment one is dishing out is appropriate. For informal social punishment to be justified, Radzik argues, four additional conditions must be met. First, the punisher must have an *accurate* take on the nature of the wrong for which the other party is being punished. If one does not know the facts of the case – moral and material – one has no business administering punishment, even if the punishment would otherwise be deserved. Second, the harm the wrongdoer suffers must be *proportional* to the severity of the wrong she committed. The punishment should also be *instrumental* in bringing about a better state of affairs. There are several worthwhile ends it could serve, such as deterring future wrongdoing, maintaining important norms, vindicating victims, maintaining self-respect, and avoiding complicity.[11] But the end it should serve, Radzik

---

[11] Linda Radzik, Chapter 2 in this volume, 40–41.

contends, is to move the wrongdoer to make amends for her transgression.[12] Even if the punishment would bring about some of these other ends, if it does not increase the chances that the wrongdoer will see the error of her ways, acknowledge her failings to the victim, and take steps to repair the harm she has caused, Radzik argues, it is unjustified. Conditions two and three both recommend a fourth condition for justified social punishment, which is a preference that it be done in *private*. Ordinarily, being called out in front of a large audience provokes more shame than a comparable confrontation conducted in private. If the punitive response takes place before an audience, others are more likely to join in the criticism, which limits the punishers' control over the degree of harm their collective actions might cause. Furthermore, when challenged in public a wrongdoer is more likely to adopt a defensive posture and less likely to acknowledge she was wrong or take other steps to make amends than she would have been in a private confrontation. Observations like these lead Radzik to suggest, "Perhaps a good provisional rule is that informal social punishments should be delivered privately unless there is a good reason to punish publicly."[13]

How does the Hart case look when evaluated against these standards? The criticisms that had the greatest impact on discussions of Hart's behavior were well documented. They included links to YouTube videos of Hart's stand-up routine and screenshots of his Twitter posts. His remarks were not misleadingly edited or presented out of context. Furthermore, it was clearly acknowledged that the most troublesome behavior was several years old: the offensive tweets and stand-up routine were from 2009, 2010, and 2011. So it would have required a special kind of inattention for those who criticized Hart or pressured the Academy to have done so based on an inaccurate sense of the wrongdoing in question. Nevertheless, Hart contested the accuracy of the criticism directed at him on the grounds that he had already apologized for the relevant comments and that even at the time he made them they did not reflect homophobic attitudes but merely insensitivity on his part. However, the earlier apologies came only after interviewers pressured him to address his comments. And they were more excuse than apology: times were different then, people are more sensitive now.[14] The original actions coupled with more recent role choices and the defensive posture he adopted in response to his

---

[12] Ibid., 41.
[13] Linda Radzik, Chapter 3 in this volume, 59.
[14] Jonah Weiner, "Kevin Hart's Funny Business," *Rolling Stone*, online edition, July 29, 2015.

critics all reveal a more serious moral failing than simple insensitivity. It seems Hart's critics have a more accurate sense of the relevant actions and attitudes than he does.

Assessing the proportionality of the response to Hart is more complicated. What is a proportional response to actions like Hart's? Questions like this have long posed a challenge for retributivists. We might try to answer it in terms of actions of the same moral type – in this case insults that feed cultural hostility toward people like Hart (celebrities? comedians? cisgender straight men? African Americans?) – but that would be unpalatable. Surely the right response to bigotry is not more bigotry, albeit of a different flavor. We might try to answer it in terms of the harm victims suffered, but this does not look any better. According to this standard, a minor misdeed (say, negligence) that affects a million people might warrant imposing a more severe punishment than a serious and malicious wrong (such as murder) that affects only one. A third option would be to try to define proportionality in terms of fitting attitudes and the actions that express them. However, if the fitting attitude is an indignation that would be optimally expressed by slapping the wrongdoer, and if the wrongful act was directed at (or visible to) a large population, then the cumulative effect of all their slaps could be excessive when compared with the severity of the transgression.

Let us assume that such worries can be addressed and that we can identify a workable account of proportionality. Given the astonishing violence that is still directed at members of the LGBTQ+ community, even in Western countries like the United States, acting in ways that foster or normalize homophobic attitudes is a serious offense. Doing so before a large audience – on stage, in film, and on a Twitter account that has 35 million followers – makes the action worse. So having a handful of critical articles appear in the press and a few thousand people tweet their disapproval does not seem a disproportional response. Nor does the Academy's demand that Hart offer a public apology. In other words, the critical response directed at Hart does not appear to be out of proportion – however that gets defined – to the seriousness of the wrong he committed.

The Hart case meets Radzik's third condition for appropriate punishment, as well. The critical response increased the likelihood that Hart would make amends. Although his initial response was defensive and he rejected the Academy's call for an apology, eventually Hart did apologize.[15] In a tweet announcing he would not be hosting the Oscars ceremony, he wrote,

---

[15] Stephen Daw, "A Complete Timeline of Kevin Hart's Oscar-Hosting Controversy, from Tweets to Apologies," *Billboard*, online edition, Jan. 10, 2019.

"I sincerely apologize to the LGBTQ community for my insensitive words from my past.... I'm sorry that I hurt people. I am evolving and want to continue to do so. My goal is to bring people together not tear us apart."[16] And he repeated the apology in an interview on Sirius XM radio a month later.[17]

Regarding the privacy condition, some of those who confronted Hart about his homophobic jokes and tweets did so in private. However, most of those who objected to Hart's actions could not have voiced their concerns to him privately. They do not have a personal relationship with him that would afford them an opportunity to speak to him alone. So even if they shared Radzik's preference for private punishment, in this context that preference could not be satisfied. Does that make the public response to Hart inappropriate? No. Privacy is not required in all cases of informal social punishment for them to be justified. It is simply preferable if the punishment can be administered out of the public eye. But on some occasions, a public response is acceptable. And since the misdeeds were very public and the only way for most people to address them was via social media, the Kevin Hart case would seem to be one such occasion.

The upshot of the discussion thus far is that Radzik has provided us with a useful way to interpret events like the response to Kevin Hart's derogatory references to being gay in his stand-up routines, tweets, and movies. However, I want to ask whether this is the best way to read cases like Hart's. I shall suggest that a more appropriate interpretation would see what people were doing as protest rather than punishment. To motivate this claim, it will be helpful to look at another recent case that shares a number of features with what Radzik calls social punishment, but that is better read as a case of protest. I shall then highlight similarities between this case and the response to Kevin Hart that suggest we should read his case differently than Radzik's analysis might recommend.

3 THE EDITOR AND THE JOURNALIST

At Waitrose, the UK-based grocery chain, 2018 could be dubbed the year of the vegan. Early in the year they launched their own line of vegan cuisine and introduced a section dedicated to vegan foods in their stores.

---

[16] Kevin Hart@KevinHart4real, *Twitter*, Dec. 6, 2018, https://twitter.com/KevinHart4real/status/1070906075812118529 and https://twitter.com/KevinHart4real/status/1070906121551007745.

[17] Trilby Beresford, "Kevin Hart Apologizes Again, Defends Past Jokes on SiriusXM Show," *Billboard*, online edition, Jan. 7, 2019.

Customer reception was so positive that in October they announced the release of another forty vegan products.[18]

Responding to this vegan-friendly turn, Selene Nelson, a freelance journalist, decided to pitch an idea for a series of articles on "plant-based" meals to the editor of *Waitrose Food* magazine, William Sitwell.

Hi William,

I hope you're well. I'm a freelance food and travel writer for *Town & Country*, *Huff Post*, *Food Republic*, *SUITCASE Magazine* etc., and I wanted to pitch an idea for a regular feature in *Waitrose Food*.

Recently there's been a huge rise in veganism, with people increasingly interested in its health and environmental benefits, as well as issues surrounding animal welfare. The popularity of the movement is likely to continue to skyrocket, and I think there's a great opportunity for *Waitrose Food* to introduce a series on vegan cooking, perhaps in a similar style to the *Guardian Weekend*'s series "The New Vegan." In January the "Veganuary" incentive is expected to be more popular than ever, and people will be keen to discover plant-based meal ideas. Even for people not looking to change their diet, I think having some more healthy, eco-friendly meals won't go amiss, particularly in the New Year! I envisage the feature including recipes as well as commentary, news, maybe with some collaborations with top vegan chefs too (I've already chatted to some who are interested).

I have lots of ideas for this but don't want to bombard you! Please let me know your thoughts – I strongly believe this would be a welcome, and timely, new addition to *Waitrose Food*. You can take a look at my portfolio here; let me know if you have any questions or want to see any further writing samples. Many thanks and I look forward to hearing from you!

Kind regards,
Selene Nelson[19]

It would be an understatement to say Sitwell was not a fan of the idea. But rather than just saying, "Thanks for the proposal, but we won't be pursuing the idea at this time," he replied as follows:

Hi Selene

Thanks for this. How about a series on killing vegans, one by one. Ways to trap them? How to interrogate them properly? Expose their hypocrisy? Force-feed them meat? Make them eat steak and drink red wine?

WILLIAM SITWELL[20]

---

[18] "Waitrose Launches Massive New Range of 40 Vegan and Vegetarian Products," *Vegan Food & Living.com*, Oct. 10, 2018.

[19] Posted on Twitter by Selene Nelson on Oct. 29, 2018 (https://twitter.com/selene_nelson?lang=en, accessed Dec. 10, 2018).

[20] Mark Di Stefano, "This Vegan Journalist Pitched to Waitrose Food Magazine, and the Editor Replied Proposing a Series about Killing Vegans," *BuzzFeed*, Oct. 29, 2018.

Needless to say, this was not the response Nelson was expecting. But she wasn't ready to give up on her proposal just yet. So she wrote back to Sitwell inviting further dialogue.

Hi William,

Thanks for your interesting response. I drank some delicious (vegan) red wine last night so I'm sure a feature on that would appeal ... I'm not quite sure what you mean by "exposing their hypocrisy," but I'm certainly interested in exploring why just the mention of veganism seems to make some people so hostile. It sounds like you have some opinions on this? I'd love to know more!

Thanks,
Selene[21]

It was a nice try; however, this was not a dialogue Sitwell was prepared to have. His flippant reply to Nelson's second email was, "I like the idea of a column called The Honest Vegan; a millennial's diary of earnest endeavour and bacon sandwiches."[22]

By now it was clear Sitwell would not be offering Nelson a job anytime soon. It was also clear that Sitwell had a prejudice against vegans. Nelson could have stewed silently about the rude treatment she had received. Instead, she decided to contact a journalist at BuzzFeed and pass along the correspondence. Before the week was out, BuzzFeed published an article with the headline, "This Vegan Journalist Pitched to Waitrose Food Magazine, and the Editor Replied Proposing a Series about Killing Vegans," which included excerpts from Nelson and Sitwell's email exchange.[23] The story was then picked up by the *Times*, the *Independent*, the *Evening Standard*, the *Telegraph*, the BBC, *Metro*, and even the *Daily Mail*. The discussion the story sparked – on blogs and comment threads, on talk radio, and around the water cooler – was highly critical of Sitwell, and Waitrose was concerned they needed to do something to protect their brand. So, less than forty-eight hours after BuzzFeed broke the story, Sitwell tendered his resignation.[24]

---

[21] Posted on Twitter by Selene Nelson on October 29, 2018 (https://twitter.com/selene_nelson?lang=en, accessed Dec. 10, 2018).

[22] Di Stefano, "This Vegan Journalist Pitched to Waitrose Food Magazine."

[23] Ibid.

[24] "Waitrose Food: Editor William Sitwell Resigns over 'Killing Vegans' Row," *BBC News*, Oct. 31, 2018.

4 UNJUSTIFIED SOCIAL PUNISHMENT

As with the Hart case, Radzik's account of informal social punishment provides a way for us to read the Sitwell case. In forwarding their correspondence to BuzzFeed, Nelson was taking steps aimed at *intentionally* imposing *harm* on Sitwell by drawing unwanted, critical attention to his anti-vegan remarks. These steps were a *reaction* to Sitwell's disrespectful and dismissive emails and were meant to *express disapproval*. Furthermore, as the recipient of this disrespectful treatment, Nelson was authorized to take such steps. So Nelson's actions fit Radzik's definition of informal social punishment. If we assume that bystanders are also authorized to criticize those who are guilty of disrespectful and prejudicial behavior, then those who weighed in on the issue in various online fora were also authorized to express disapproval in reaction to Sitwell's anti-vegan bias. Consequently, their actions would also count as informal social punishment. And since Waitrose was authorized to scold or even dismiss one of its employees for workplace behaviors they deemed unprofessional and harmful to their brand, their actions would count as formal social punishment in Radzik's taxonomy.

However, if we turn our attention to whether such social punishment was justified, the Sitwell case fares less well. The problem is not with the accuracy of people's judgments about what Sitwell did. As with the Hart case, the details of what took place were widely and accurately reported. Certainly, Nelson and Waitrose had a reliable grasp of the facts of the situation. And while some readers may have skimmed the news rather hastily and missed some of the relevant details, most of those who added their voice to the online discussion of Sitwell's actions would have had a reasonably accurate sense of what he had done.

One might wonder how instrumental Nelson et al.'s actions were likely to be in bringing Sitwell to apologize and take steps to correct his attitude toward vegans or, at least, his treatment of them. First, the tone adopted in his exchange with Nelson was not out of character. For example, reviewing the year's new cookbooks for the *Times* in January 2018, Sitwell wrote, "Then, like an avalanche of Tory ministerial resignations, came the vegan snowball. It had slow beginnings among shampoo-averse hippies in the 1970s, but now vegans are parking their tanks on all of our lawns. And their instruction manuals are coming like propaganda pamphlets dropping from the sky. The publisher Quadrille is pumping out Gaz Oakley's *Vegan 100* and Katy Beskow's *15-Minute Vegan Comfort Food* (presumably you gnaw on celery for 15 minutes, then have a dinner of roast chicken and apple crumble)."[25] He continues his anti-vegan rant throughout the piece, adding memorable lines such as, "There's nowt so toothless as a booze-free, this-century vegan."[26] Second, this was not the first time he had been called out regarding his jaundiced portrayal of veganism. After his piece in the *Times*, a number of contributors to the online discussion thread pushed back against his caricature of vegans and vegan cuisine. For example, "endless sea" wrote, "bit old hat laughing at vegans eating celery etc. If you want to be very healthy and lean you can do worse than be vegan. It is also good for animal welfare and the environment. (I am not a vegan.)"[27] Shamala Govindasamy made a similar point: "Very disappointed to read the prejudiced comments about vegans only eating celery and the cookbooks labelled as propaganda. It's tiresome, unfair and outdated."[28] A number of other comments expressed similar sentiments. Third, as noted above, when called out in public, people often become more defensive and are therefore less likely to apologize or seek to make amends.

However, as it turned out, Nelson's decision to make their correspondence public did prove instrumental to Sitwell apologizing. When he announced his resignation on Instagram, he offered an apology, "to any food- and life-loving vegan who was genuinely offended by remarks written by me as an ill-judged joke."[29] He wrote Nelson a six-page letter in which he apologized to her. And when he and Nelson met with BBC reporter Justin Rowlatt, a few weeks later, he reiterated that he was sorry for how he had responded to her emails.[30] It is unclear how much Sitwell's attitude has shifted: in the segments of his meeting with Nelson that the BBC posted online, the criticisms of veganism he voiced were still built on caricatures of the position. But in light of the public outcry at his remarks, it is probable that at least his future behavior will change. He is unlikely to speak of vegans in the same prejudicial way in future articles or emails. So Nelson's and the wider public's response may pass the instrumental test, as well.

When we turn our attention to proportionality, however, the case looks more problematic, and this is in large part because the punishment was not administered privately. There were individuals whose actions clearly were

---

[25] William Sitwell, "Dumplings and Vegan Double Acts: The Foodie Trends of 2018," *The Times*, online edition, Jan. 4, 2018.
[26] Ibid.
[27] Ibid.
[28] Ibid.
[29] William Sitwell, "William Sitwell Meets the Woman Who Called Him Out for 'Vegan-Killing' Comments: This Time I'd 'Gone Too Far,'" *The Telegraph*, online edition, Jan. 27, 2019.
[30] "Waitrose's Ex-'Killing Vegans' Editor Meets Vegan," *BBC News*, online edition, Nov. 26, 2018.

disproportionate to the wrong in question. After BuzzFeed published the story, Sitwell received a number of hostile messages from readers, including one that recommended fattening up his two-month-old child and roasting him.[31] But even those whose reactions were more tempered might worry that the cumulative effect of the critical public scrutiny exceeded what Sitwell deserved.

Veganism has not been treated as a flawed, perverted, or wicked way of life. Religious traditions have not vilified vegans. Indeed, important strands within many religious traditions have taken veganism to be admirable or even obligatory. Vegans have not faced widespread bullying, nor have they been killed for their veganism. There have been no laws prohibiting the practice of veganism or barring vegans from marrying whom they want or occupying desirable social roles. And referring to others as vegans has not been a commonly used form of insult. So Sitwell's remarks, although in some sense more outrageous than Hart's, were read against different background assumptions. Both were jokes in poor taste, but there was no worry that Sitwell or anyone else might actually consider cooking vegans, whereas the same could not be said for Hart's jokes about breaking a doll house over a son's head to curb his gayness. Sitwell's jokes were dismissive, rather than denigrating. And neither giving someone the brush-off nor portraying a group of people as self-righteous or hypocritical is the kind of offense that warrants public criticism from thousands of people and the termination of one's employment.

It is not surprising, then, that Sitwell's resignation was met with an outpouring of sympathy. A number of people argued he was a nice guy who had an off day, whose punishment was completely out of proportion to his actions, and who was now the victim of political correctness run amok.[32] Mark Paul, for example, wrote that Sitwell was "harshly driven from his job . . . by a salivating online mob . . . Veganism's online hounds from hell went in search of a human sacrifice."[33] Even Nelson – who received an abundance of equally nasty correspondence and public criticism after Sitwell resigned – indicated she was sorry he lost his job, suggesting that she too thought it was a worse outcome than his actions warranted. Thus, if we read the Nelson–Sitwell case as an instance of informal social punishment, then the actions of Nelson and those who

---

[31] Sabrina Barr, "Vegans Threatened to 'Roast My Baby,' Former Waitrose Magazine Editor Claims," *The Independent*, online edition, Nov. 26, 2018.
[32] See Jacob Jarvis, "Former Waitrose Food Magazine Editor William Sitwell 'Makes Up' with Vegan Freelancer Who Cost Him His Job," *The Standard*, online edition, Nov. 27, 2018.
[33] Mark Paul, "Why Do Companies Debase Staff by Throwing Them to the Wolves?," *The Irish Times*, online edition, Nov. 1, 2018.

joined her in criticizing Sitwell would appear to be unjustified, and they ought to have refrained from acting as they did.

5 PROTEST

The preceding sections show that the responses to Kevin Hart and William Sitwell can be read as instances of what Linda Radzik calls informal social punishment. And in each case, that informal social punishment led to formal social punishment in the form of a loss of employment for the punished party. However, in one case, Hart's punishment was on the whole justified; whereas in the other, Sitwell's punishment appears on the whole unjustified. I say, "on the whole," to allow room for the odd individual whose response was inappropriate. And I say, "appears" because I do not pretend to have considered all the factors that have an evaluative bearing on these cases. What matters for my purposes is that the sketch I have offered provides a reasonable idea of how the concept and associated standards of informal social punishment can be used to interpret familiar events like the reactions on social media to Hart's and Sitwell's words.

However, I want to propose an alternative reading of each case that highlights similar features but yields different normative conclusions. Instead of interpreting them as instances of punishment, I recommend reading them as examples of protest. And protests, I contend, are governed by different norms.

The defining feature of a protest is that it *rejects its object*. That object can take more forms than punishment's object. Whereas punishment is directed at an agent for a moral failing for which they are responsible, protest can be directed at a claim (expressed or implied), a behavior, an attitude, an assumption, a rule, a system, or a way of life. Whatever its object, a protest insists that its object is not okay as it stands. Furthermore, protest *expresses* this rejection. Merely thinking "not X" in response to X is not yet to protest against X. That thought must also be expressed in action.

When we reflect on examples of protest, we tend to imagine large, public marches in which chants, placards, and speeches clearly articulate what is being rejected. However, a protest need not express its rejection so overtly.[34]

---

[34] 'Protest' can refer to an action type, an instance of that type, or an event in which actions of that type predominate. For stylistic reasons I use the term in each of these ways, since it makes no difference to the substance of the argument. Which use I am making of 'protest' at which time should be clear from the context.

There are silent as well as vocal forms of protest.[35] For instance, on learning that a company damages its natural environment or exploits its employees, a consumer's protest may take the form of refusing to purchase its products until it changes its business practices.[36]

The sort of rejection a protest expresses is more than simple disagreement or factual correction. Bernard Boxill suggests that what distinguishes protest from these other actions is that protest expresses resentment.[37] While I am happy to agree that this is often the case, building resentment into the definition of protest as a necessary feature would rule out actions that we would ordinarily want to call instances of protest. Take, for example, the Put It to the People rally held in London on March 23, 2019, to protest the May government's refusal to allow its citizens to vote on the deal she negotiated for the withdrawal of the United Kingdom from the European Union. Someone who made a sign that read "Forget the Ides of March – Beware the Brexit of May!" which they carried over their head as they marched through London chanting "Let us vote" would be engaged in protesting. And this would be true even if they were a Buddhist or a Stoic who had spent years taming their emotions so that they never expressed resentment or any other form of anger. A better way to capture the feature that distinguishes mere disagreement from protest is that the latter involves *disapproval* of the object, assumption, claim, action, or system being rejected and of the person(s) responsible for it. If this is right, then, like punishment, protest reproves those who exemplify what it rejects.

Another way in which protesting is like punishing is that it is *intentionally* done. One cannot inadvertently protest: the pedestrian whose destination happens to lie in the same direction that a protest march is traveling and whose speed matches theirs is not engaged in protest if his only intention in walking with them is to reach that destination. The difference between punishing and protesting concerns what they intentionally do. Whereas punishing, on Radzik's view, involves intentionally harming its object, protesting involves intentionally rejecting its object.

Protest, like punishment, involves exerting *power* against its object. In this respect it, too, fits Mill's description of our response to wrongdoing: "When we think that a person is bound in justice to do a thing ... we

[35] Thomas E. Hill Jr., "Symbolic Protest and Calculated Silence," in *Autonomy and Self-Respect* (New York: Cambridge University Press, 1991), 52–66.
[36] See Radzik, Chapter 2 in this volume.
[37] Bernard Boxill, "Self-Respect and Protest," *Philosophy and Public Affairs* 6, no. 1 (1976): 58–69, at 61.

should be gratified to see the obligation enforced by anybody who had the power."[38] Ideally, but not necessarily, the power that protest brings to bear on a situation will be sufficient to end the objectionable system or behavior. In an even more ideal world, it will be sufficient to change the attitude or assumption that was exemplified in the objectionable behavior or system. But neither protest nor punishment, in themselves, are concerned with whether the alteration in the behavior or system is brought about by an internal change in motivation or an external change in incentives.

To this point I have emphasized some of the similarities between protest and punishment. But there are also a number of respects in which they are markedly different. Perhaps the most striking difference between protest and punishment concerns the power relations that exist between the parties. Punishment is meted out by someone who holds at least as much power as the one punished, usually more. The social relations between a protestor and the one at whom the protest is directed, by contrast, are typically the reverse. That is why the disapproval takes the form of a protest, rather than a rebuke. Consequently, for a protest to achieve its aim of altering the behavior, attitude, or system in question, it must tap into some other power source. That source of power can be internal to an agent whose behaviors or attitudes the protestor would like to change, connecting with their emotions or providing them with reasons they find persuasive. But often the power source is external. To overcome the disparity in power, the protestor needs to recruit a more powerful ally or harness the collective power of a like-minded group.

As noted above, protest can be directed not only at individual actions but also at commonplace and systemic problems. However, when protesting systemic problems, it is often necessary to shine a spotlight on a particular instance of the larger problem as a way of giving the systemic quality a face. There are three reasons for this. The first is evidential: the best way to provide evidence of a systemic problem is to offer examples of individual cases that exemplify the broader pattern. The second is pedagogical: in order to understand the nature of a systemic problem, one must look at particular instances. The third is rhetorical: people are more easily persuaded to stand against a problem with a name and a face than they are to resist a problem that is more abstractly defined.

---

[38] John Stuart Mill, *Utilitarianism*, in *Collected Works of John Stuart Mill*, ed. J. M. Robson, vol. 10 (Toronto: University of Toronto Press, 1969), V.13.

Because protest can take a systemic problem as its object, *protest need not be "reactive" to the transgression of someone who is responsible for what is being rejected.*[39] In the case of systemic problems, like racism, it may not matter how "guilty" the party is whose actions are taken to exemplify the problem. Whether they endorse the system or they merely illustrate its influence may not be significant. For example, someone might post a photo of the teaching staff of a philosophy department along with the caption, "Look. A collection of white men. It must be a philosophy department." Such an action would highlight a systemic problem that needs to be addressed by the discipline as a whole. And this would be true – and the protest warranted – even if each of the people included in the photo had just been hired and none had done anything remotely objectionable in their pursuit of employment.[40]

Relatedly, *protest need not be proportional* to the wrong instantiated in the individual action that is its focal point. There are various ways in which one might attempt to reintroduce proportionality. For example, one might think protest should be proportional to the good that would be achieved were the protest successful. However, such a standard seems to set the bar too low. In protesting racial injustice in the pre–civil rights era in Alabama, Martin Luther King Jr. and those who marched with him clearly dreamed big. They hoped that one day their children would "live in a nation where they will not be judged by the color of their skin but by the content of their character."[41] At the same time, they recognized that their protest would not accomplish that aim. Theirs was but a step in a much longer journey – one whose conclusion we still await. Yet when it comes to determining whether their protest would be justified, it surely makes sense to appeal to the good of full racial equality – even if it is only a dream that is still several decades off and depends on thousands of other actions – rather than limiting our attention to the good they could reasonably expect a particular protest to achieve. This suggests a more capacious standard for justified protest: it should not exceed the magnitude of the evil being opposed or the good being defended.

While we have been considering one respect in which the norms governing the harms that result from protest are more permissive than

[39] This is true even if we use the broad sense of responsibility for which Cheshire Calhoun argues in "Responsibility and Reproach," *Ethics* 99, no. 2 (1989): 389–406.
[40] Thanks to Paul Christopher Morrow for suggesting this example.
[41] Martin Luther King Jr., "I Have a Dream (1963)," in *A Testament of Hope: The Essential Writings and Speeches of Martin Luther King, Jr.*, ed. James M. Washington (New York: HarperCollins, 1986), 217–20, at 219.

those governing punishment, it should be noted that protest need not be harmful at all to those at whom it is directed. The members of the abovementioned philosophy department might fully embrace the concern on which the protest is based. And they might join their voices to those already raised in protest. Indeed, protest need not even be *intended* to harm.

Neither need protest be instrumentally effective. Some arguments are worth having even if we cannot hope to persuade our opponent, and some powers worth resisting regardless of whether there is a chance of success against them. In such circumstances, W. E. B. DuBois advised, "even when bending to the inevitable," one should "bend with unabated protest."[42] Why? Because the point of protest is not just to change that at which (or at whom) the protest is directed. It can also be to express self-respect,[43] to maintain one's honor or integrity,[44] to declare one's allegiance to the good, or to speak truth to power, calling injustice or wickedness by its proper name.

Since the instrumentality and proportionality constraints that govern punishment do not apply in the case of protest, the reasons Radzik offers for preferring that social punishment be administered in private do not apply, either, because the latter is derived from the former. But insofar as one of protest's aims is to end the problematic attitudes and behaviors to which it objects, a similar argument can be constructed in favor of private protest, at least in some cases. However, some of protest's other aims – like expressing self-respect, preserving one's honor, supporting the downtrodden, and declaring one's allegiance to the good – would be thwarted by privacy. Moreover, protesting systemic evils generally requires publicity. Why? Typically, systemic evils are public.[45] The systems in question may be constructed out of and maintained by the actions of private individuals acting in private. The actors in question need not even understand the system in which they participate (although they often only pretend not to understand it). Even so, the harms they cause are public, social harms. They distribute public burdens and benefits unfairly, they destroy lives, they undermine public trust. A second reason that protesting systemic evils

---

[42] W. E. B. DuBois, "The Parting of the Ways," in *W. E. B. DuBois*, ed. William Tuttle Jr. (Upper Saddle River, NJ: Prentice Hall 1973), 43, quoted in Boxill, "Self-Respect and Protest," 62.
[43] Boxill, "Self-Respect and Protest"; and Matthew Talbert, "Moral Competence, Moral Blame, and Protest," *Journal of Ethics* 16 (2012): 89–109, at 105–7.
[44] Jean Harvey, "Oppression, Moral Abandonment, and the Role of Protest," *Journal of Social Philosophy* 27, no. 1 (1996): 156–71, at 160.
[45] I am grateful to an anonymous referee for encouraging me to expand this point.

requires publicity is that correcting those evils requires large-scale changes by those with a vested interest in keeping things the way they are. Initiating such a change requires considerable power, and characteristically the victims of systemic evil are in a less powerful social position than those who maintain the current system. As noted above, countering that power differential requires either enlisting more powerful allies or generating collective power by banding together with other victims of the system, usually both. Doing either of those things usually involves visible, public action. Consequently, the preference for privacy will apply to a much narrower range of protests than punishments.

Finally, the authorization conditions for protest differ from those that apply to punishment. There are interesting questions about whether violent protest is ever justified, but I shall assume that even if it is, those who are engaged in violent protest are not authorized to do so. In most political contexts, the only party authorized to use violence is the state, so that will not be where the authorization conditions of social punishment and protest come apart. Rather, the place they diverge has to do with who has the authority to participate in the activity of punishing or protesting per se. Radzik argues quite plausibly that someone who is constantly guilty of a particular kind of transgression lacks the authority to punish someone else for a similar infraction. The same does not appear true of protest. Someone who is guilty of prejudicial actions against group A still retains the authority to protest similar prejudicial actions against group B. The fact that he is biased against Mexican Americans or Vietnamese Americans does not mean a black man lacks the authority to protest the bias against African Americans that is all too common in American society. Indeed, he could even show prejudice against African Americans himself – perhaps by unconsciously preferring to hire white applicants to fill jobs in his company – without losing the authority to protest such prejudice when he sees it in others. Doing so may make him a hypocrite. It may also undermine the persuasive force of his protest if it is known. But it does not disqualify him from protesting the wrongs he sees, even if there are many similar wrongs to which he is blind.

6 THE EDITOR AND THE COMEDIAN

Now that we have an account of protest to work with, let us return to the cases we discussed in Sections 1 and 3. When Nelson forwarded her correspondence with Sitwell to the journalist at BuzzFeed, she was intentionally expressing her disapproval of the way in which he had treated both her, in particular, and vegans more generally. Furthermore, the power in the relationship all rested with Sitwell – she was the prospective employee, he the employer; she was a member of the cultural minority, he of the majority; she was a lower-paid woman, he a better-paid man; she was relatively unknown, he a well-known member of a popular television program – so for her protest to be effective she needed to recruit more powerful allies, which in this case was served by appealing to the public. And insofar as Sitwell's remarks were illustrative of a hostility toward vegans that is surprisingly common in the United Kingdom, the prejudice she was rejecting was not merely an individual problem. So calling out this instance of bad behavior would also serve the purpose of highlighting a problem that has received insufficient attention. Nelson's actions, then, look like a textbook case of protest. And read as an act of protest, both she and those who added their voices to hers on social media sites were justified. Even if the dietary, ethical, and environmental reasons in support of veganism were not persuasive, the hostility that gets directed at vegans is uncalled for. Vegans are already at a disadvantage relative to the rest of UK society. Most restaurants do not have a vegan option on the menu. Those that do, typically have only one, and it is seldom the dish that exemplifies the chef's creative talents. Vegans also have a very limited range of packaged foods from which to choose at the supermarket and even fewer beers and wines that are suitable for their consumption. The point of these observations is not to argue that vegans are treated unjustly by restaurants, grocery stores, or food manufacturers. It is simply to note that for reasons of conscience they are willing to give up a range of conveniences and pleasures their peers enjoy. Other things being equal, we should not make it harder for people to act in accordance with conscience, nor should we tell derogatory jokes about them because we are offended by their conscientiousness.[46] If, on the other hand, ethical or environmental reasons support veganism – whether across the entire population or within a growing segment of it – then hostility toward them is especially egregious and ought to be rejected quite vocally. Either way, the good being defended would justify the kinds of actions taken by Nelson and most of those who took up her cause.

If we turn our attention to the Hart case, we see that it, too, can be read as protest. When Lee first tweeted about Hart, he was intentionally expressing his disapproval of the homophobia that is still present in the

---

[46] Of course, if someone's "conscientious" action causes another undeserved harm, then "other things" are not equal. But that concern does not apply to the case in question.

United States and of the Academy's decision to make someone whose actions contribute to that culture the face of its biggest event. Those who joined the online criticism of Hart's homophobic remarks or of the Academy for choosing him to host the Oscars ceremony were likewise protesting a widespread problem in the United States and urging the Academy to underscore the fact that homophobia is not okay. And given how serious homophobia continues to be in most countries around the world, including the United States, outspoken criticism in newspapers and online is more than justified.

Each of these cases, then, can be read both as protest and as punishment. If read as protest, each appears to be warranted. If read as punishment, only one of them is justified. How do we decide which way to read these events? One approach would be to appeal to ordinary language, but since "informal social punishment" is a term of art that Radzik is just introducing, that would give protest an unearned advantaged. An alternative would be to leave it to the object of the reprobative action to decide. However, this would be an odd standard, insofar as it would leave it to the wrongdoer to decide (a) whether she was in the wrong and (b) how her wrongdoing should be treated. The practical upshot would be that most instances of protest would collapse into punishment. Kevin Hart, William Sitwell, Vladimir Putin, Donald Trump, Theresa May, and the majority of others whose actions or attitudes have been cause for protest will feel as though they are being subjected to undeserved harm. And the more systemic the evil, the more likely the perpetrators are to think their actions innocent. A third approach would appeal to the attitudes of those engaged in the activity of protesting or punishing. Since punishment involves intentional harming and protest intentional rejecting, we might try to identify the action by way of the intention. The problem with this proposal is that intentional rejecting and intentional harming are not mutually exclusive categories. In many cases, an agent will intend to do both by way of the same action. And even if, counterfactually, every individual involved acted with just one of these intentions, it would nevertheless be the case that in actions like those we have been considering, which include thousands of individuals, the same problem would recur at a collective level. Finally, if all punishment expresses a rejection of the kind of behavior being punished and a disapproval of the person responsible, as Radzik suggests, then every instance of punishment will also be a case of protest.

Thus, we have a distinction between two overlapping concepts. But at the point of overlap we lack a principled way of deciding whether we should read a situation through the lens of the first concept or the second. Since this distinction makes a moral difference, it would be good to have a principled way of deciding which to employ. Consequently, more work needs to be done, either (a) to refine (or replace) the concepts to reduce the overlap, (b) to identify reasons for giving one concept priority over the other, or (c) to explain how one fills the gap between justified protest/ punishment and justified action.

PART III

Replies

CHAPTER 7

Response to Bennett, Sher, and Pettigrove

Linda Radzik

I INTRODUCTION

It is a privilege to write something and have three eminent scholars dedicate their talents to critiquing and improving it. Below, I show my appreciation to Christopher Bennett, George Sher, and Glen Pettigrove by answering their main questions and challenges to the best of my ability. Each of their essays was originally written as a direct response to one of the chapters and focuses on the themes of that chapter: defining social punishment, justifying social punishment, and the application of these ideas to our practices, respectively. My replies will follow this same structure.

2 RESPONSE TO BENNETT ON THE DEFINITION OF PUNISHMENT

Below, I focus on four main issues raised in Bennett's essay. First, he argues that my definition of punishment is vulnerable to counterexample because it treats the five defining conditions as separate elements. Second, he defends David Shoemaker's stronger interpretation of the harm condition in the definition of punishment, which requires a form of harming that would otherwise violate a right were it not for the transgression. Third, Bennett suggests that the authority to punish may make sense only as part of a more complex right, which social equals in everyday life are unlikely to possess. Fourth, Bennett presents an alternative account of punishment, which interprets it as primarily a kind of expressive action.

2.1 Combining the Elements in the Definition of Social Punishment

Bennett is correct to point out that the definition of social punishment that I defend in Chapter 1 is inadequate. In arguing that social punishment is authorized, intentional, reprobative, reactive harming, I present each of the five elements as if they were separate items on a checklist. But, as

Bennett demonstrates, this argumentative strategy leaves me unable to draw a distinction between social punishments and mere natural penalties. Following Mill, I argue that my merely avoiding a person who drinks too much does not count as punishing that person.[1] Instead, I am simply exercising my liberty in a different direction. Yet, as Bennett notes: (1) my avoidance may well harm the drunkard; (2) it is a reaction to his drinking; (3) my "judgment of disapproval is in some sense *expressed* in my avoidance"; (4) I act intentionally in avoiding this person; and (5) I am not failing to mind my own business in avoiding the drunkard.[2] So, this paradigmatic case of a natural penalty presents a counterexample to my definition of punishment.

The lesson of Bennett's critique here is that "we must pay attention to the *specific* way in which these conditions are *combined* in punishment."[3] So, I would like to amend the definition of punishment that I provided by clarifying the scope of the intention condition and emphasizing the centrality of the harm condition. Punishments are cases of harming that are intentionally harmful, intentionally reactive, and intentionally reprobative, as well as being authorized. When a brother punishes his sister for telling a malicious lie by avoiding her, he intends to harm her; he intends to impose this harm on her in order to respond to her misdeed; and he intends for this imposition of harm to express his reprobation. Furthermore, the brother is not failing to mind his own business in doing these things.

These changes to the definition of punishment allow me to maintain the distinction between social punishments and mere natural penalties. In the earlier example, my avoidance of the excessive drinker harms him, but I am not intentionally (i.e., both knowingly and purposely) harming him. My purpose is not to set back his interests in any way but simply to spend my time in more pleasant company. My avoidance is a reaction to his behavior in the sense that his behavior prompts my choice. However, I am not intentionally responding to his action in the way that giving an answer intentionally responds to someone who asks a question, or waving back responds to a wave. Although my avoidance expresses that I have a negative attitude toward his drinking in the sense that an observer might well be able to interpret my attitude from my behavior, my purpose in avoiding

[1] John Stuart Mill, *On Liberty*, in *Collected Works of John Stuart Mill*, vol. 18, ed. J. M. Robson (Toronto: University of Toronto Press, 1977), IV.6.
[2] Christopher Bennett, Chapter 4 in this volume, 80.
[3] Ibid., 81.

him is neither to vent such disapproval nor to communicate that disapproval to others, but only to spend my time differently. Finally, the sort of authority that I need in this case is simply the authority to choose where and with whom I spend my time, whereas in the example of punishment, the brother requires the authority to intentionally harm his sister in order to respond with reprobation to her misdeed.

2.2 The Harm Condition and the Question of Rights

On another point of definition, Bennett suggests that I too quickly dismiss Shoemaker's strong interpretation of the harm condition. Shoemaker claims that an action does not count as punishment unless it imposes the sort of harm that would violate a right were it not for the alleged misdeed of the one being punished.[4] The key counterexample to Shoemaker's claim is that parents surely count as punishing children when they ban them from playing video games or send them to bed early, yet children have no right to play video games or stay up to a certain hour. Gaming access and bedtimes are matters of parental discretion. While Bennett agrees that such examples of parental punishment do not violate fundamental moral or legal rights, he argues that they do suspend "reasonable normative expectations, or perhaps even entitlements, regarding . . . goods and freedoms."[5]

I agree that these cases of parental punishment involve violations of what would be (absent the wrong) reasonable normative expectations. The children in the examples have reasonable expectations about their bedtimes and gaming options, given their parents' past behaviors, and that is part of why they experience early bedtimes and gaming bans as harmful. But I hesitate to describe the children as having entitlements to these things (at least, absent any explicit promises from the parents). Entitlements are rights-claims and rights-claims strike me as too strong.

But the question of whether punishment involves the violation of what would otherwise be a right resurfaces in Chapter 2, where I turn from the project of defining social punishment to that of justifying it. At that point, I give in to the temptation to interpret informal social punishments as violating what would otherwise be a right – namely, a moral right not to be subjected to the intentional manipulation of one's emotions and choice

---

[4] David Shoemaker, "Blame and Punishment," in *Blame: Its Nature and Norms*, ed. D. Justin Coates and Neal A. Tognazzini (New York: Oxford University Press, 2013), 100–118, at 115.
[5] Bennett, Chapter 4 in this volume.

options. As Sher correctly points out, though, this move saddles me with the unenviable task of distinguishing between violations of this alleged moral right and innocent interactions such as negotiating with one's spouse about what to watch on television.[6] Bennett's suggestion that social punishment more generally violates what would otherwise be a right to respect and concern faces similar line-drawing challenges.[7]

Sher's critique leads me to believe I should have followed my first impulse to avoid rights-talk. The harms involved in punishment need not touch on rights. Formal and informal social punishments frequently do not touch on rights, although they often violate reasonable normative expectations. When the brother punishes his sister for lying by avoiding her at family gatherings, and does so with the goal of morally pressuring her to atone, he does not violate her rights. But he does act contrary to her expectations to be greeted with openness and warmth, expectations that have previously formed part of the fabric of their relationship. It is also fair to say that he behaves in a way for which he would deserve criticism were it not for his sister's transgression. When he violates these expectations, he intentionally hurts her feelings. Were it not for her misdeed, the brother would have wronged his sister by so doing. We can say all of these things without making claims about rights or entitlements.

2.3 Authority as a Complex Right

Bennett also makes some interesting comments about the authority to punish. He notes that in the case of legal punishment, the state's authority to enforce the law through punishment is combined with its authority to legislate and its authority to adjudicate how legislation applies to particular cases. Bennett suggests that the state possesses enforcement authority *because* it is part of a "complex right" that includes both legislative and judicial authority.[8] In other words, the example of the state may lead us to believe that the authority to punish must accompany these other forms of authority if it is to be legitimate. If so, then in order to defend the claim that social equals sometimes have the authority to punish one another for moral wrongdoing, I would have to argue further that social equals have the authority not only to adjudicate moral claims but also to legislate morality. This would be a daunting – and many would say, unappealing – task.

---

[6] George Sher, Chapter 5 in this volume, 147.
[7] Bennett, Chapter 4 in this volume, 85.
[8] Ibid., 87–88.

Bennett suggests that this might provide me with a reason for substituting the language of the "authority" to punish with admittedly vague language about "standing" to punish.

Bennett raises deep questions here about the nature and source of authority, which I am not prepared to engage fully. However, his analysis of state authority does not worry me much at this stage. While he is correct that the state considered as a whole unit does have enforcement, judicial, and legislative forms of authority, many states divide those forms of authority among independent parts of the government. The legislatures that make the laws are distinct from the court systems that apply the laws and the prison systems that carry out sentences. So the separation or distribution of these forms of authority, such that one party might possess the authority to punish without having these other forms of authority, strikes me as coherent. Consider as well punishment carried out by religious communities where the laws in question are believed to be set by God, not by the community itself.

In earlier work, I used the word 'standing' in exploring questions about who may overtly express reprobation in response to wrongdoing and who should instead mind their own business.[9] In this book, I decided to replace the term with 'authority' because issues of standing in the law are quite different from what I am interested in here.[10] In the civil law, having standing merely gives one the right to bring an issue to court (e.g., to sue another party for damages or to ask for an injunction). It does not entitle one to enforce the law or punish lawbreakers. For this reason, I prefer to phrase the questions about who is permitted to punish as questions about authority rather than standing.

2.4 Punishment as Expressive Action

In addition to these specific critiques, Bennett's essay develops an alternative perspective on the topic of social punishment. Bennett approaches actions such as moral criticism, rebuke, and pointed social withdrawal as points on a continuum of responses to wrongdoing that satisfy various social needs. In the latter half of his essay, Bennett follows a genealogical methodology, providing a "speculative, developmental story" about how

---

[9] Linda Radzik, "On Minding Your Own Business: Differentiating Accountability Relations within the Moral Community," *Social Theory and Practice* 37, no. 4 (2011): 574–98.

[10] Marilyn Friedman, "How to Blame People Responsibly," *Journal of Value Inquiry* 47, no. 3 (2013): 275–82, at 277–78.

such practices of responding to wrongdoing might have emerged within a community where members have interests in developing a set of shared rules, principles, and values; educating and socializing one another into these normative systems; defending these values against violations; communicating ideas and values with one another; and managing emotions.[11] Bennett argues that "[e]xpressive needs and social control needs . . . help to constitute our sense of obligation" and that then, in turn, we come to see ourselves as obliged to express our values, including by punishing wrongdoing.[12]

According to Bennett's interpretation, as I understand it, punishment is a ritual action that marks a transgression as wrong and thereby symbolically does justice to our value-rich interpretations of the world. Earlier in the chapter, Bennett writes that "it is essential to punishment that hard treatment is imposed *thereby* to convey disapproval."[13] Punishments (though not only punishments) "involve a form of behavior toward a perceived wrongdoer that is such as to *mark* their behavior as wrongful."[14] Furthermore, "in punishment the hard treatment *means* disapproval."[15]

In other words, for Bennett, punishment is primarily a kind of expressive action, whereas I see punishment as primarily a kind of intentional harming. I agree with Bennett that punishment is also expressive, and he agrees with me (I think) that punishment is also intentionally harmful. But the difference in emphasis is significant.

Although I find much appealing and promising in Bennett's genealogical account, I worry about the emphasis it gives to the point of view of the ones doing the punishing. The discussion highlights the social and expressive needs of the ones imposing the harms rather than the interests of those being harmed. While this may succeed as a genealogical account of how such practices *emerge*, I worry that it sets us up to elide the interests of the ones being punished when we move on to questions of justification. It may lead us to approach the task of justifying punishment as the task of showing that it is intelligible. But surely the weightier question is whether it is morally permissible given the fact that it involves the intentional harming of another person.

---

[11] Bennett, Chapter 4 in this volume, 89–98.
[12] Ibid., 93.
[13] Ibid., 82.
[14] Ibid., 83.
[15] Ibid., 86.

3 RESPONSE TO SHER ON THE JUSTIFICATION OF SOCIAL PUNISHMENT

George Sher's essay also raises far too many interesting questions than I can possibly pursue here. I respond to just three of the objections he raises to the account of the justifying aim of informal social punishment that I defend in Chapter 2. First, Sher argues that the moral pressure theory does not succeed in differentiating my version of the desert element from the traditional, retributivist version that I condemn as bloodthirsty. Second, Sher objects to my suggestion that the desert element can be reformulated in terms of rights-forfeiture. Third, he points out that the instrumental element in my theory does not clarify how effective informal social punishment would have to be in motivating atonement in order for the punishment to be justified.

3.1 Desert of Suffering

Sher's weightiest objection is that I do not manage to create any daylight between my version of a desert element in punishment and the traditional, pure retributivist view. Sher writes,

> Because she has these objections [to the bloodthirstiness of the pure retributivist view], Radzik confronts a difficult task. On the one hand, she must explain how past wrongdoing can play a role in justifying social sanctions, but on the other, she must do so without endorsing the suffering that those sanctions inflict.[16]

But this summary of my predicament is not quite right. I do endorse making people suffer in some cases. After all, I have claimed that punishment is sometimes justified and that punishment, by definition, involves harm. Harm typically brings suffering, which we might think of as a painful subjective experience. What I reject is that the suffering is justified in virtue of its being intrinsically desirable that wrongdoers suffer.

I now think that framing the debate as one over the "object of desert," as I do in Chapter 2, is an obstacle to finding the daylight between my position and pure retributivism. The "object of desert" language papers over an important distinction between *justificandum* and *justificans*. In any theory of justification, the *justificandum* is that which stands in need of justification. The *justificans* is the thing that does the justifying. To illustrate the distinction, consider the debate about epistemic justification.

---

[16] Sher, Chapter 5 in this volume, 102.

The *justificandum* – the thing that stands in need of justification – is a belief, for example, a perceptual belief such as, "There is a cat." The *justificans* is whatever provides that justification. Epistemologists have a provided a number of different candidates for the *justificans* in cases like these. Externalists appeal to things like the objective reliability of the believer's perceptual system. Internalists point to other mental states that provide just the right kind of inferential support for the belief in the cat. Some epistemologists even believe that simple perceptual beliefs are self-justifying, though defeasibly so. The idea here is that the very occurrence of beliefs like "There is a cat" provides sufficient though defeasible evidence that there is, in fact, a cat present.[17] The belief is both the *justificandum* and the *justificans*.

In Chapter 2, the *justficandum* is informal social punishment, which involves an intentional infliction of harm on alleged wrongdoers. An intentional infliction of harm is, at least frequently and predictably, an intentional infliction of suffering. Suffering is always prima facie morally worrying. So, suffering and harm are what stand in need of justification. Pure retributivists and I agree about this. Where we disagree is that pure retributivists believe that suffering is also the *justificans*. They believe that inflicting suffering on wrongdoers is justified *because it is suffering*. That they will suffer is a sufficient though defeasible reason for inflicting suffering on them. This tight connection between the *justificandum* and the *justificans* is captured by the thought that the suffering of the guilty is intrinsically justified or that it has a positive valence in itself. Their suffering is what we aim to achieve; it is the valuable end that conveys value to acts of punishment. This is the view that I find bloodthirsty.

In my account of informal social punishment, suffering is a *justificandum* but not a *justificans*. The infliction of suffering on wrongdoers is sometimes justified, but the suffering is not itself the source of the justification. The justifying reason for punishing wrongdoers is not *the intrinsic goodness of their suffering*. Instead, the wrongdoers' loss of liberty justifies their suffering. Wrongdoers have misused their will. They have misused their liberty. In the aftermath of wrongdoing, then, there is something intrinsically fitting or good or desirable in their losing a degree of liberty through the curtailment of their wills.[18] In my view, the intrinsic

---

[17] John L. Pollock and Joseph Cruz, *Contemporary Theories of Knowledge*, 2nd ed. (Lanham, MD: Rowman and Littlefield, 1999), ch. 2. The belief might be defeated by other beliefs, such as "I am currently in a hologram laboratory" or "I recently ingested a hallucinogen."

[18] This language resembles that of Herbert Fingarette, who also takes seriously the challenge of defending punishment while avoiding the repugnant claim that there is something intrinsically

fittingness of such a loss of liberty provides a justifying reason for punishing wrongdoers (though not a sufficient justifying reason).[19] Suffering is deserved, one might be tempted to say, because the curtailment of the will is deserved. The experience of being subjected to interference from others predictably brings suffering. However, the suffering is not itself the intrinsically desirable good that justifies punishment.

This, then, is my revised attempt to distinguish my account of desert from that of the pure retributivist. Whereas the pure retributivist sees suffering as both *justificandum* and *justificans*, I see suffering as *justificandum* but not *justificans*. But on this point, I face another objection from Sher. What I have said so far suggests that suffering is a mere side effect curtailing the wrongdoer's liberty. However, he objects that

coercion of this kind works precisely because it *does* involve the infliction of (a minor form of) suffering. To bring this out, we need only ask ourselves why anyone should *care* about not being embarrassed, shamed, reprimanded, called out, censured, or shunned. The obvious answer . . . is that we want to avoid these forms of treatment because we find them *unpleasant*.[20]

In punishing, we curtail the wrongdoer's will *by* inflicting suffering. Suffering is not just a side effect; it is the *means* by which we limit the wrongdoer's liberty.

I used this same pattern of criticism in objecting to theorists who attempt to justify punishment as a form of communication. Suffering is not merely the side effect of receiving a deserved condemnation, I argued. The imposition of suffering is also the means by which the message is sent. Part of the reason why this objection is compelling against the communicative theorist is that there seem to be *other ways* of sending messages to people that are less harmful than punishment. We might engage in mere moral criticism or resort to Joel Feinberg's imagined rituals of music and dance.[21] The end can

desirable about the wrongdoer's pain. He suggests that the wrongdoer deserves a "humbling" of the will. But whereas Fingarette offers this concept as an interpretation of the *kind of suffering* that is characteristic of punishment, I am suggesting that we see the limitation of the will as the thing that is deserved and the imposition of suffering or other forms of harm as the means of achieving such a limitation. Herbert Fingarette, "Punishment and Suffering," *Proceedings and Addresses of the American Philosophical Association* 50, no. 6 (1977): 499–525. Thanks to Jeffrie Murphy for urging me to consider Fingarette's view.
[19] Like other mixed theorists, I argue that both negative desert and good consequences are required for the justification of punishment.
[20] Sher, Chapter 5 in this volume, 105.
[21] Joel Feinberg, "The Expressive Function of Punishment," in *Doing and Deserving: Essays in the Theory of Responsibility* (Princeton: Princeton University Press, 1970), 95–118, at 116.

be satisfied without resorting to the use of harmful means, and so the use of harmful means is not justified. Or so I argued.

Similarly, if the aim of curtailing the wrongdoer's will can be achieved without punishing (i.e., without intentionally inflicting a harm on her that intentionally expresses reprobation as a response to her actions), then such means should be preferred. But what would the alternative look like? I have argued that the characteristic harms of informal social punishment are emotional distress and the limitation of the wrongdoer's choice options. Any intentional decision to curtail her liberty will involve a decision to limit her choice options. However, if we can proportionately limit her liberty without also intentionally inflicting (as much) emotional pain, then we should. But this is only an argument against unnecessarily harsh punishments, not against punishing as such.

My opponent might reply that these considerations recommend merely natural penalties over informal social punishment. For example, if I believe my niece has been a negligent caretaker to my young child, then I should simply refrain from hiring her to babysit again in the future instead of also intentionally causing her emotional distress with a rebuke. My aim would not be to curtail her will, but merely to choose the best care for my child. Yet my decision would still predictably result in a deserved loss of liberty for my niece, including the loss of a job opportunity and the chance to bond with her cousin, but without my having to purposefully bring such losses about. Interestingly, however, the rebuke might actually be less harmful than the natural penalty. In rebuking my niece, I would also be giving her the opportunity to defend herself or make amends, and perhaps win back the babysitting job and good relations with her family. The rebuke purposely imposes something on her she would prefer not to experience, but it leaves her with more valuable options than the natural penalty. Sometimes, at least, informal social punishment will be the less harmful way for the wrongdoer to receive her just deserts.

3.2 Rights Forfeiture

In Chapter 2, I suggest that the desert element in the moral pressure account, which holds that wrongdoers deserve both a loss of liberty and an expression of censure,[22] could be restated as a version of a rights-forfeiture theory. The idea was that, in committing a moral transgression, the

---

[22] I did not mention the claim that wrongdoers deserve censure in the last section for the sake of simplicity. I have not changed my mind about the importance of this idea.

wrongdoer forfeits some degree of his liberty. I then claimed that this is equivalent to saying that he forfeits a right not to be emotionally pressured or to have his choice options intentionally manipulated. Sher rightfully points out how difficult it would be to defend the claim that we have any such right or to define the boundaries of such a right.

Do I really have a right not to be subjected to the intentional manipulation of my emotions? If I do, isn't it violated daily by advertisers, political candidates, panhandlers, charity mailers, and everyone else who uses rhetoric instead of reason to get me to believe something? ... Am I wronged when the supermarket intentionally limits my options to not getting English muffins and paying $2.49 for them? Does my wife violate my rights when she makes it clear that she won't watch the ball game with me unless I watch *Better Call Saul* with her?[23]

As I mentioned in my response to Bennett, I now concede that rights language is too strong. The kind of liberty that is forfeited in wrongdoing is not always the sort that entails rights claims on other people's non-interference. So, the justification for punishment that I offer is not well described as a type of rights-forfeiture theory.

However, I do think that the harms imposed in informal social punishment typically violate what would otherwise be the reasonable expectations of the ones punished. What counts as a reasonable expectation is highly context-sensitive and relative to the relationships between the parties. Customers reasonably expect supermarkets to demand money in return for their products. A wife who says, "I will watch the game with you only if you watch my favorite show with me," does nothing objectionable, as it is reasonably to be expected that couples will negotiate with one another about how they spend their time together. On the other hand, a wife who refuses to remain in the same room with her husband does violate her husband's reasonable expectations. Yet in neither case does the wife violate a right.

3.3 The Effectiveness of Informal Social Punishment

In the second half of his essay, Sher focuses on the instrumental element in the moral pressure theory of punishment. I argue that, in order to be justified, informal social punishment must aim to pressure the wrongdoer to make amends. I also say that the making of amends requires, among

---

[23] Sher, Chapter 5 in this volume, 103–4.

other things, the moral improvement of the wrongdoer. Sher objects that
I offer no evidence that these are realistic goals.

> First, to link social punishment to the making of amends, [Radzik] must establish
> that moral pressure standardly or typically *leads* to wrongdoers making amends;
> and, second, to link the making of amends to moral improvement, she must
> establish that those who make amends always or usually become morally better as
> a result.[24]

Sher emphasizes that "each is, in the end, a claim about how the world
works."[25]

Sher is correct that Chapter 2 offers no empirical evidence on either of
these two questions: whether informal social punishment tends to motivate the making of amends, or whether the making of amends through
methods such as apology tends to lead to long-term moral improvement.
I am unable to offer any such evidence now. Chapter 2 also fails to clarify
the more conceptual issue of *how effective* these things would have to be in
order to justify the use of informal social punishment. I knowingly left this
point vague simply because I was – and remain – uncertain about how it
would be best to fill in this detail.

While I cannot answer Sher's main objections here, I would like to add
a few comments. Most importantly, I am not pro-punishment. My project
in these chapters is not to advocate social punishment or recommend that
we punish more frequently. Should empirical studies of informal social
punishment reveal that it rarely motivates people to make amends and
improve themselves, then I will be content to conclude that informal social
punishment is rarely justified. Instead of punishing, we should then find
other ways to respond to wrongdoing, such as moral criticism or
persuasion.

If such alternative methods leave people too vulnerable to wrongdoing,
then I would replace the instrumental element in my account with one
focused on deterrence. This would yield a familiar version of a mixed
theory, according to which informal social punishment would be justified
only if the ones punished are guilty of wrongdoing and punishing them
would be effective (to some degree here unspecified) in deterring them or
others from committing such wrongs in the future. But such a world
would be morally worse than one in which atonement and moral improvement are realistic goals. Call me an optimist, but I bet that we can aim

higher than mere deterrence with our practices of informal social punishment. If we can aim higher, then we should because doing so embodies a richer form of respect for one another.

I predict that empirical studies of informal social punishment are likely to reveal that effectiveness, both in inspiring amends and in deterring wrongdoing, will not be directly correlated with the harshness of penalties. As Sher observes, "when someone threatens to make things unpleasant for us if we do not do as he says, our natural first reaction is not to align our will with his, but rather to view his demand as an unwelcome imposition."[26] Aggression may inspire only counteraggression. I suspect that the most effective forms of social punishment will be ones that find just the right mix of harmful and communicative elements, such that the harms tend to draw attention to reasons for acting morally rather than to distract the wrongdoer with her own suffering. Effective social punishments are likely to be those forms of harming that remind the wrongdoer how beneficial it is to live on terms of respect and goodwill with the punishers, rather than those which turn the punishers into objects of fear and distrust. In our example of the brother and his lying sister, it is plausible that his sullen avoidance of her at family events would be more effective in inspiring her to make amends than a humiliating, shouted rebuke in front of their relatives.

4 RESPONSE TO PETTIGROVE ON THE INTERPRETATION OF OUR PRACTICES

Glen Pettigrove's essay provides an insightful comparison between socially punishing and protesting.[27] Below, I point out how this distinction may provide an attractive alternative for thinking through the difficult cases I present at the end of Chapter 3. I agree with Pettigrove that how we interpret particular responses to wrongdoing has ramifications for our judgments about their permissibility. An action that would be unjustified as an instance of social punishment could yet be justified as an instance of protest. How, then, should we go about fixing on a particular interpretation? What sorts of standards should guide our classification of specific actions? While I offer a few thoughts on this below, I am unable to answer these questions at this time. Instead, I complicate the terrain even further by arguing that we should split Pettigrove's category of protest into

---

[26] Ibid., 110.
[27] Glen Pettigrove, Chapter 6 in this volume.

additional categories, which differ from each other as much as they differ from social punishment.

Chapter 3 ends on a rather tortured note. The latter half of the chapter examines the #MeToo and #LivingWhileBlack social media campaigns, which publicly name and shame people alleged to have committed gender- and race-based forms of harassment. I argued that, in at least some of these cases, the harms experienced by the wrongdoers (which include public humiliation, loss of employment, and damage to reputation that is likely to be long-lasting and unresponsive to any future moral improvement) may be disproportional to the offense and present obstacles to the wrongdoers making amends. For these reasons, the moral pressure theory that I advocate would classify these as unjustified acts of social punishment. Yet I argued further that these actions might be justified all things considered, given the moral urgency of the project of dismantling gender- and race-based forms of oppression, and the difficulty of finding alternative means of doing so. In other words, I suggested that these cases might count as justified exceptions to the moral pressure theory of social punishment. Some members of the audience at the Descartes Lectures, as well as other readers with whom I have shared this material, are uneasy with this conclusion. The worry is that it permits treating wrongdoers worse than they deserve. It permits wronging them in service of a greater end.

The theory of protest that Pettigrove develops provides us with an alternative model for analyzing these cases. Instead of seeing them as problematic cases of social punishment, we might instead interpret them as unproblematic cases of protest. Indeed, the #MeToo and #LivingWhileBlack examples include the key features that Pettigrove associates with paradigmatic cases of protest. The wrongs being opposed (the specific acts of sexual and racial harassment) are parts of larger patterns of injustice. The victims of the wrongs occupy less powerful social positions than do the wrongdoers. Furthermore, the victims cannot reliably utilize alternative, effective means of receiving redress. Instead, in order to exert power in the situation, the protestors "must tap into some other power source," either by persuading the target of the protest or by recruiting other parties to add their means of influence to those of the protestors.[28]

Pettigrove writes that, "Whereas punishing, on Radzik's view, involves intentionally harming its object, protesting involves intentionally rejecting

---

[28] Ibid., 127.

its object."[29] Protest "rejects its object" in the sense that it intentionally expresses that "its object is not okay as it stands."[30] Protest communicates "disapproval."[31] Protest also "involves exerting *power* against its object . . . Ideally, but not necessarily, the power that protest brings to bear on a situation will be sufficient to end the objectionable system or behavior."[32] But protests may be justified even when they have no hope of ending injustice.

One way of understanding the distinction between social punishment and Pettigrove's conception of protest is by attending to the target of the action. Social punishment targets the wrongdoer; protests typically instead target a larger injustice. While a protest may be most immediately directed at a specific unjust actor (e.g., a specific harasser is named and shamed), the actor is simply the face of the larger problem.

This conceptual reframing of naming and shaming shifts the moral principles according to which it should be judged, Pettigrove argues. Considerations of proportionality between the wrong and the response will still be relevant. But now the question is not whether the harms of the naming and shaming exceed the negative desert of the person specifically named. Instead, the relevant comparison is between the severity of the protest and the severity of the larger injustice that is the real target of the protest, or perhaps the significance of the good that is being defended. Another difference is that the justifiability of a protest does not depend on its instrumental value. A protest may have no chance of curtailing injustice. Instead, its justification is rooted in the role it plays "to express self-respect, to maintain one's honour or integrity, to declare one's allegiance to the good, or to speak truth to power, calling injustice or wickedness by its proper name."[33]

Pettigrove is right to emphasize questions of interpretation here. One and the same set of behaviors can be interpreted as different actions, and these different actions may well be subject to different standards of evaluation. Indeed, elsewhere I have argued that paradigmatic cases of consumer boycott admit of at least four possible interpretations, each

[29] Ibid., 126.
[30] Ibid., 125.
[31] Ibid., 127.
[32] Ibid., 126–7.
[33] Ibid., 129.

of which raises distinct issues about justification.[34] Boycotters may be simply avoiding complicity in wrongdoing, engaging in protest speech, socially punishing, or engaging in social coercion. I briefly summarize these categories here in order to compare them with Pettigrove's conception of protesting.

Paradigmatic boycotts involve avoiding or withdrawing from consumer or cultural activities in response to some sort of transgression by the one being boycotted. Sometimes, the point of the withdrawal is simply to avoid complicity in wrongdoing. For example, the point of boycotting environmentally destructive agricultural products need not be to inflict harm on the farmer but to avoid contributing to a particular set of environmental ills. Here, the harm to the one being boycotted is neither the direct nor indirect goal of the boycotter's action; instead, the harm is simply a foreseeable side effect.

In most cases, however, much of the point of boycotting is overtly to communicate a message of disapproval of the target. I associate the term 'protest speech' with this sort of action. So, I would say that most boycotts are protests. However, boycotts send their moral messages *by doing something else*, namely, avoiding or withdrawing from consumer or cultural activities. So, boycotts are rarely merely speech acts.

The third possible frame for interpreting boycotts is as social punishment. As Chapters 1–3 explain, I see social punishment as tied up in all sorts of complex ways with condemnatory speech. An act is not punishment unless there is an expression of reprobation. Furthermore, when punishment is justified, part of the aim is to communicate a set of moral judgments and demands to the wrongdoer. Communication with a broader audience is sometimes part of the goal as well. But punishment is also an action that intentionally inflicts harm on the wrongdoer. Harming the wrongdoer is a direct intention of the action, although it ought not be the ultimate aim. When performed well, the ultimate goal is to pressure the wrongdoer to make amends, or so I have argued.

The fourth interpretive frame locates boycotts under a broader category of social coercion. Social coercion inflicts, or threatens to inflict, undesirable consequences on someone with the goal of pressuring her to make a certain choice. In "A Letter from Birmingham Jail," Martin Luther King Jr. writes that the purpose of his marches and boycotts is to force his

---

[34] Linda Radzik, "Boycotts and the Social Enforcement of Justice," *Social Philosophy & Policy* 34, no. 1 (2017): 102–22.

opponents to the negotiating table.[35] "Nonviolent direct action seeks to create such a crisis and foster such a tension that a community which has constantly refused to negotiate is forced to confront the issue," he writes.[36] While punishments are typically forms of coercion insofar as they aim to influence future behavior, not all forms of coercion are also cases of punishment. For example, threats of punishment are coercive but not punitive. The norms regulating coercion are also distinguishable from those regulating punishment. While punishment may be applied only to the guilty, threats of punishment may be aimed at both the guilty and the innocent with an eye to deterring future wrongdoing. Furthermore, the standards of proportionality that properly limit coercion differ in complex ways from those that regulate punishment. For example, punishment accumulates over time. A small punishment repeated over a long period adds up, eventually becoming proportionate to the wrong or harm and rendering more punishment inappropriate. But a small amount of coercive pressure might remain appropriate to the issue in question, no matter how long it has been applied.

Pettigrove's conception of protest certainly bears many similarities to my category of protest speech. Recall Pettigrove's examples of the naming and shaming of magazine editor William Sitwell for his derogatory comments about vegans and comedian Kevin Hart for his homophobic jokes. According to Pettigrove, in these cases, the protestors aim to communicate disapproval of the larger phenomena of anti-vegan hostility and homophobia. So, these protests count as speech acts. But what, precisely, was the specific function of focusing these protests on Sitwell and Hart in particular? After all, the protestors could have sent condemnatory messages about the larger injustices without tying those messages to these men's names, let alone pressing for them to be fired. For some protestors, the focus on Sitwell or Hart may simply have been in service to the project of communicating the moral message. As Pettigrove puts it,

when protesting systemic problems, it is often necessary to shine a spotlight on a particular instance of the larger problem as a way of giving the systemic quality a face. There are three reasons for this. The first is evidential: the best way to provide evidence of a systemic problem is to offer examples of individual cases

---

[35] Martin Luther King Jr., "Letter from Birmingham Jail (1963)," in *A Testament of Hope: The Essential Writings and Speeches of Martin Luther King, Jr.*, ed. James M. Washington (New York: HarperCollins, 1986), 289–302.
[36] Ibid., 291.

that exemplify the broader pattern. The second is pedagogical: in order to understand the nature of a systemic problem, one must look at particular instances. The third is rhetorical: people are more easily persuaded to stand against a problem with a name and a face than they are to resist a problem that is more abstractly defined.[37]

Sitwell and Hart were harmed, Pettigrove suggests, but harming them was not the direct point of the protest; moral communication was. Still, it is worth highlighting that publicly shaming Sitwell and Hart and calling for them to be fired were not merely foreseeable side effects of the main communicative act. They were the means by which the communication was achieved, as Pettigrove's analysis here makes clear. In my opinion, while these namings and shamings were certainly cases of protest speech, they were not merely cases of protest speech. The protestors sent their messages by doing something else.

As Pettigrove's own analysis highlights, the protestors in these cases were not merely engaging in moral communication; they were also exercising power against Sitwell and Hart. The protesters joined together in order to exercise power in defense of victims who are often comparatively powerless, as individuals, to defend their own interests. To what end was this power exercised? It might have been to socially punish Sitwell and Hart or to socially coerce them into better behavior (or both). But another alternative is that the goal was to socially coerce anti-vegans and homophobes *in general* by threatening them with similar consequences should they also act on their prejudices. On this interpretation, the harms inflicted on Sitwell and Hart were not the main aim of the naming and shaming campaigns; they were, instead, the means used to fight a larger injustice by threatening other people into better behavior. So the protests against Sitwell and Hart can be interpreted as protest speech, but they seem also to be cases of either social punishment or social coercion.

So, how do we settle on the proper interpretation of those engaged in actions such as naming and shaming or boycotts? Surely, we do not want to encourage actors to simply select whichever framework gives them the green light to do what they want to do anyway. While I do not have satisfactory answer to this question, I would like to offer a few thoughts.

Insofar as our task is to morally evaluate the actions of the people engaging in public shaming or boycotts, it seems reasonable to place

---

[37] Pettigrove, Chapter 6 in this volume, 127.

quite a bit of weight on the content of their intentions. Is the actor intending to communicate a message of disapproval, to harm the specific wrongdoer, or to issue a threat to a wider audience? We should be prepared for cases in which the answer is not one of these three but some combination of them. Communicating moral messages, punishing wrongdoers, and issuing broader threats may all form part of the actors' intentions. However, as Pettigrove also notes, the actors' intentions should not fully settle the question of interpretation. For one thing, their intentions may not be fully articulate or they may change over time. Ascribing intentions to groups of individuals working together also presents problems. More importantly, the actors' self-understanding may impermissibly ignore the consequences that they create for the target, or how the target reasonably interprets their actions. The meanings of our actions are at least partly socially constructed.

So, we should also take the effects of a boycott or social media campaign into account when considering how best to classify the action. For example, where there is little chance that a boycott will affect the bottom line of a huge corporation, viewing it as protest speech is preferable to viewing it as social coercion. The coercive pressure applied is too small to be morally significant. In another case, the boycotters may aim to punish a business by inflicting financial harm on it, but instead wind up helping the target by providing the business with free publicity, which leads to increased sales. Here, the boycott fails as punishment, although it might succeed in enabling the protestors to avoid complicity.

I agree with Pettigrove that particular responses to wrongdoing often admit of alternative interpretations and that these alternative interpretations will often make some justificatory standards more relevant than others. However, I doubt that simply shifting our conceptual scheme will settle the difficult questions about hard cases, such as those that occupied me in Chapter 3. The Sitwell case, as well as some of the #MeToo and #LivingWhileBlack cases, involve harms to wrongdoers that exceed their own negative desert. Whether we interpret the naming and shaming campaigns as acts of protest speech, social coercion, or social punishment, we run into the same fundamental moral objection. The protestors are knowingly harming particular individuals in excess of their desert in service of some other end. Under the protest speech interpretation, the end is to broadcast a moral message. Under the social coercion interpretation, the end is to pressure people in general into changing their behavior. Under the social punishment interpretation, the end should be to pressure the wrongdoers to make amends for their misdeeds, but also to deter wrongdoing in general. In all three versions of the cases, the fundamental problem is the same. No matter which end we choose, harming wrong-doers in excess of their personal desert treats them as mere means. The fundamental tension between respecting the individual and pursuing the greater good remains. Once we see this, the importance of the question of interpretation fades. The truly difficult problem lies in deciding when it is permissible, or perhaps excusable, to sacrifice the claims of the individual to the greater good.

Bibliography

Anderson, Scott. "Coercion." In *Stanford Encyclopedia of Philosophy*, ed. Edward N. Zalta, 2017. plato.stanford.edu.

Aquinas, St. Thomas. *Summa Theologica*. Trans. Fathers of the English Dominican Province. Project Gutenberg, 2006.

Baker, Brenda M. "Penance as a Model for Punishment." *Social Theory and Practice* 18, no. 3 (1992): 311–31.

Barr, Sabrina. "Vegans Threatened to 'Roast My Baby,' Former Waitrose Magazine Editor Claims." *The Independent*, Nov. 26, 2018.

Bell, Macalester. "The Standing to Blame: A Critique." In *Blame: Its Nature and Norms*, ed. D. Justin Coates and Neal A. Tognazzini, 263–81. New York: Oxford University Press, 2012.

Benn, Stanley I. "Punishment." In *The Encyclopedia of Philosophy*, ed. Paul Williams. Vol. 7, 29–36. New York: Macmillan, 1967.

Bennett, Christopher. *The Apology Ritual*. New York: Cambridge University Press, 2008.

"The Authority of Moral Oversight: On the Legitimacy of Criminal Law." *Legal Theory* 25, no. 3 (2019): 153–77.

"Expressive Actions." In *The Expression of Emotion*, ed. C. Abell and J. Smith, 73–94. Cambridge: Cambridge University Press, 2016.

"The Expressive Function of Blame." In *Blame: Its Nature and Norms*, ed. D. Justin Coates and Neal A. Tognazzini, 66–83. New York: Oxford University Press, 2013.

"How Should We Argue for a Censure Theory of Punishment?" In *Penal Censure: Engagements within and beyond Desert Theory*, ed. Antje du Bois-Pedain and Anthony E. Bottoms, 67–84. Oxford: Hart, 2019.

"Penal Disenfranchisement." *Criminal Law and Philosophy* 10 (2016): 411–25.

"Review of David Owens' *Shaping the Normative Landscape*." *Jurisprudence* 6 (2015): 364–70.

"The Varieties of Retributive Experience." *The Philosophical Quarterly* 52, no. 207 (2002): 145–63.

Bentham, Jeremy. *The Principles of Morals and Legislation*. Buffalo, NY: Prometheus Books, 1988.

Beresford, Trilby. "Kevin Hart Apologizes again, Defends Past Jokes on SiriusXM Show." *Billboard*, online edition, Jan. 7, 2019.

Blackmon, Michael. "Kevin Hart Is Deleting Old Anti-Gay Tweets after Being Announced as Oscars Host." *BuzzFeed*, Dec. 6, 2018.

Boonin, David. *The Problem of Punishment.* New York: Cambridge University Press, 2008.

Boxill, Bernard R. "Self-Respect and Protest." *Philosophy and Public Affairs* 6, no. 1 (1976.): 58–69.

Braithwaite, John. "Repentance Rituals and Restorative Justice." *Journal of Political Philosophy* 8, no. 1 (2000): 115–31.

Calhoun, Cheshire. "Responsibility and Reproach." *Ethics* 99, no. 2 (1989): 389–406.

Clarke, Randolph. "Some Theses on Desert." *Philosophical Explorations* 16, no. 2 (2013): 153–64.

Cogley, Zac. "Basic Desert of Reactive Emotions." *Philosophical Explorations* 16, no. 2 (2013): 165–77.

Cohen, G. A. "Casting the First Stone: Who Can, and Who Can't, Condemn the Terrorists?" *Royal Institute of Philosophy Supplement* 58 (2006): 113–36.

Cook, Michael. *Commanding Right and Forbidding Wrong in Islamic Thought.* New York: Cambridge University Press, 2000.

Cooper, Brittney. "How Free Speech Works for White Academics." *The Chronicle of Higher Education* 64, no. 13 (2017): 8.

Cushman, Fiery. "Punishment in Humans: From Intuitions to Institutions." *Philosophy Compass* 10, no. 2 (2015): 117–33.

Darwall, Stephen. "Justice and Retaliation." *Philosophical Papers* 39, no. 3 (2010): 315–41.

"Reply to Korsgaard, Wallace, and Watson." *Ethics* 118, no. 1 (2007): 52–69.

The Second-Person Standpoint: Morality, Respect and Accountability. Cambridge, MA: Harvard University Press, 2006.

Daw, Stephen. "A Complete Timeline of Kevin Hart's Oscar-Hosting Controversy, from Tweets to Apologies." *Billboard*, Jan. 10, 2019.

Detel, Hanne. "Disclosure and Public Shaming in the Age of New Visibility." In *Media and Public Shaming: Drawing the Boundaries of Disclosure*, ed. Julian Petley, 77–96. New York: I. B. Tauris, 2013.

Di Stefano, Mark. "This Vegan Journalist Pitched to Waitrose Food Magazine, and the Editor Replied Proposing a Series about Killing Vegans." *BuzzFeed*, Oct. 29, 2018. www.buzzfeed.com.

DuBois, W. E. B. "The Parting of the Ways." In *W. E. B. DuBois*, ed. William Tuttle Jr. (Upper Saddle River, NJ: Prentice Hall, 1973).

Duff, R. A. *Punishment, Communication, and Community.* New York: Oxford University Press, 2001.

Trials and Punishments. New York: Cambridge University Press, 1991.

Edmundson, William. "Civility as Political Constraint." *Res Publica* 8, no. 3 (2002): 217–29.

Feinberg, Joel. "The Expressive Function of Punishment." In *Doing and Deserving: Essays in the Theory of Responsibility*, 95–118. Princeton: Princeton University Press, 1970.

Harm to Self: The Moral Limits of the Criminal Law. Vol. 3. New York: Oxford University Press, 1989.

"Justice and Personal Desert." In *Doing and Deserving: Essays in the Theory of Responsibility*, 55–94. Princeton: Princeton University Press, 1970.

Fingarette, Herbert. "Punishment and Suffering." *Proceedings and Addresses of the American Philosophical Association* 50, no. 6 (1977): 499–525.

Flaspohler, Paul D., Jennifer L. Elfstrom, Karin L. Vanderzee, Holli E. Sink, and Zachary Birchmeier. "Stand by Me: The Effects of Peer and Teacher Support in Mitigating the Impact of Bullying on Quality of Life." *Psychology in the Schools* 46, no. 7 (2009): 636–49.

Flew, Antony. "The Justification of Punishment." *Philosophy* 29, no. 11 (1954): 291–307.

Fortin, Jacey. "R. Kelly's Two-Decade Trail of Sexual Abuse Accusations." *New York Times*, May 10, 2018.

Fricker, Miranda. "What's the Point of Blame? A Paradigm-Based Explanation." *Noûs* 50 (2016): 165–83.

Friedman, Marilyn. "How to Blame People Responsibly." *Journal of Value Inquiry* 47, no. 3 (2013): 275–82.

Galston, William A. "On the Alleged Right to Do Wrong: A Response to Waldron." *Ethics* 93, no. 2 (1983): 320–24.

Guala, Francesco. "Reciprocity: Weak or Strong? What Punishment Experiments Do (and Do Not) Demonstrate." *The Behavioral and Brain Sciences* 35, no. 1 (2012): 1–15.

Hampton, Jean. "Correcting Harms versus Righting Wrongs: The Goal of Retribution." *UCLA Law Review* 39, no. 6 (1992): 1659–702.

"The Moral Education Theory of Punishment." *Philosophy and Public Affairs* 13, no. 3 (1984): 208–38.

Hart, H. L. A. "Prolegomenon to the Principles of Punishment." In *Punishment and Responsibility*, 2nd ed. New York: Oxford University Press, 2008.

Harvey, Jean. "Oppression, Moral Abandonment, and the Role of Protest." *Journal of Social Philosophy* 27, no. 1 (1996): 156–71.

Hax, Carolyn. "Boom Chicka Pop to That." *Washington Post*, Oct. 26, 2017.

"Nicknaming Awesomeness: Carolyn Hax Live." *Washington Post*, Sept. 8, 2017.

"'Strangers on a Train' Except with Carpooling Instead of Murder." *Washington Post*, May 25, 2018.

Hill, Thomas E., Jr. "Symbolic Protest and Calculated Silence." In *Autonomy and Self-Respect*, 52–66. New York: Cambridge University Press, 1991.

Hume, David. *A Treatise of Human Nature*. New York: Oxford University Press, 2000.

Hursthouse, Rosalind. "Arational Actions." *The Journal of Philosophy* 88, no. 2 (1991): 57–68.

Jaffe, Klaus. "Evolution of Shame as an Adaptation to Social Punishment and Its Contribution to Social Cohesiveness." *Complexity* 14, no. 2 (2008): 46–52.

Jarvis, Jacob. "Former Waitrose Food Magazine Editor William Sitwell 'Makes Up' with Vegan Freelancer Who Cost Him His Job." *The Standard*, online edition, Nov. 27, 2018.

Jordan, Mary. "The Latest Sign of Political Divide: Shaming and Shunning Public Officials." *Washington Post*, June 24, 2018.

King, Martin Luther, Jr. "I Have a Dream (1963)." In *A Testament of Hope: The Essential Writings and Speeches of Martin Luther King, Jr.*, ed. James M. Washington, 217–20. New York: HarperCollins, 1986.

  "Letter from Birmingham Jail (1963)." In *A Testament of Hope: The Essential Writings and Speeches of Martin Luther King, Jr.*, ed. James M. Washington, 289–302. New York: HarperCollins, 1986.

Lanier, Jaron. 2018. *Ten Arguments for Deleting Your Social Media Accounts Right Now*. London: Bodley Head.

Lee, Benjamin. "Oscar Host Kevin Hart's Homphobia Is No Laughing Matter." *The Guardian*, Dec. 5, 2018.

Locke, John. "A Letter Concerning Toleration." In *John Locke on Politics and Education*. Roslyn, NY: Walter J. Black, 1947.

  Second Treatise of Government. New York: Prometheus Books, 1986.

Lucas, J. R. "Or Else." *Proceedings of the Aristotelian Society* 69 (1968): 207–22.

Matravers, Matt. "Duff on Hard Treatment." In *Crime, Punishment, and Responsibility*, ed. R. Cruft, M. Kramer, and M. Reiff, 68–86. New York: Oxford University Press, 2011.

McCarty, Alma. "'ID Adam': Man Who Questioned Black Woman's Right to Use Pool Loses Job." *USA Today*, July 7, 2018.

McCloskey, H. J. "The Complexity of the Concepts of Punishment." *Philosophy* 37, no. 142 (1962): 307–25.

McLeod, Owen. "Desert." In *Stanford Encyclopedia of Philosophy*, ed. Edward N. Zalta, 2008. plato.stanford.edu.

McNealy, Jasmine E. "The Emerging Conflict between Newsworthiness and the Right to Be Forgotten." *Northern Kentucky Law Review* 39, no. 2 (2012): 119–35.

Mill, John Stuart. *On Liberty*. In *Collected Works of John Stuart Mill*, ed. J. M. Robson. Vol. 18. Toronto: University of Toronto Press, 1977.

  Utilitarianism. In *Collected Works of John Stuart Mill*, ed. J. M. Robson. Vol. 10. Toronto: University of Toronto Press, 1969.

Mills, Claudia. "Should We Boycott Boycotts?" *Journal of Social Philosophy* 27, no. 3 (1996): 136–48.

Murphy, Jeffrie G. *Punishment and the Moral Emotions*. New York: Oxford University Press, 2012.

Murphy, Jeffrie G., and Jean Hampton. *Forgiveness and Mercy*. New York: Cambridge University Press 1988.

Nagel, Thomas. "Concealment and Exposure." *Philosophy and Public Affairs* 27, no. 1 (1998): 3–30.

Nietzsche, Friedrich. *Thus Spake Zarathustra*. Trans. Thomas Wayne. New York: Algora, 2003.

Norton, Michael I., and Samuel R. Sommers. "Whites See Racism as a Zero-Sum Game That They Are Now Losing." *Perspectives on Psychological Science* 6, no. 3 (2011): 215–18.

Owens, David. *Shaping the Normative Landscape*. Oxford: Oxford University Press, 2012.

Owens, Ernest. "Obama's Very Boomer View of 'Cancel Culture.'" *New York Times*, online edition, Nov. 1, 2019.

Paul, Mark. "Why Do Companies Debase Staff by Throwing Them to the Wolves?" *The Irish Times*, online edition, Nov. 1, 2018.

Phillips, Kristine. "A Black Lawmaker Was Canvassing Door to Door in Her District. A Constituent Called 911." *Washington Post*, July 6, 2018.

Pollock, John L., and Joseph Cruz. *Contemporary Theories of Knowledge*, 2nd ed. Lanham, MD: Rowman & Littlefield, 1999.

Queally, James. "$828,000 Raised for Indiana Pizzeria That Said It Won't Cater Gay Weddings." *Los Angeles Times*, Apr. 3, 2015.

Radzik, Linda. "Boycotts and the Social Enforcement of Justice." *Social Philosophy and Policy* 34, no. 1 (2017): 102–22.

"Bystanders and Shared Responsibility." In *Routledge Handbook of Collective Responsibility*, ed. Deborah Tollefsen and Saba Bazargan-Forward. New York: Routledge, 2020.

"Desert of What? On Murphy's Reluctant Retributivism." *Criminal Law and Philosophy* 11, no. 1 (2017): 161–73.

"Gossip and Social Punishment." *Res Philosophica* 93, no. 1 (2016): 185–204.

Making Amends: Atonement in Morality, Law, and Politics. New York: Oxford University Press, 2009.

"Moral Rebukes and Social Avoidance." *The Journal of Value Inquiry* 48, no. 4 (2014): 643–61.

"On Minding Your Own Business: Differentiating Accountability Relations within the Moral Community." *Social Theory and Practice* 37, no. 4 (2011): 574–98.

Raz, Joseph. *Practical Reason and Norms*. Oxford: Oxford University Press, 1975.

"Promises and Obligations." In *Law, Morality and Society: Essays in Honour of H. L. A. Hart*, ed. P. M. S. Hacker and Joseph Raz, 210–28. Oxford: Clarendon Press, 1977.

"Voluntary Obligations and Normative Powers: Part II." *Proceedings of the Aristotelian Society* 46 (1972): 79–102.

Ronson, Jon. *So You've Been Publicly Shamed*. New York: Riverhead Books, 2015.

Rowbottom, Jacob. "To Punish, Inform, and Criticise: The Goals of Naming and Shaming." In *Media and Public Shaming: Drawing the Boundaries of Disclosure*, ed. Julian Petley, 1–18. New York: I. B. Tauris, 2013.

Rueb, Emily S., and Derrick Bryson Taylor. "Obama on Call-Out Culture: 'That's Not Activism.'" *New York Times*, online edition, Oct. 31, 2019.

Scanlon, T. M. "Giving Desert Its Due." *Philosophical Explorations* 16, no. 2 (2013): 101–16.

Moral Dimensions: Permissibility, Meaning, Blame. Cambridge, MA: Belknap/ Harvard University Press, 2008.

Schoeman, Ferdinand David. *Privacy and Social Freedom.* New York: Cambridge University Press, 1992.

Seelye, Katharine Q., Julie Turkewitz, Jacky Healy, and Alan Blinder. "How Do You Recover after Millions Have Watched You Overdose?" *New York Times,* Dec. 25, 2018.

Selk, Avi. "In a Very Dark Sketch, SNL Points Out We Still Don't Know How to Talk about Aziz Ansari." *Washington Post,* Jan. 2, 2018.

Sharf, Zack. "Kevin Hart Called Out for Homophobic Jokes after Being Named 2019 Oscars Host." *Indie Wire,* Dec. 5, 2018.

Sher, George. *Beyond Neutrality: Perfectionism and Politics.* Cambridge: Cambridge University Press, 1997.

Shoemaker, David. "Blame and Punishment." In *Blame: Its Nature and Norms,* ed. D. Justin Coates and Neal A. Tognazzini, 100–118. New York: Oxford University Press, 2013.

Shugerman, Emily. "Me Too: Why Are Women Sharing Stories of Sexual Assault and How Did It Start?" *The Independent,* Oct. 17, 2017.

Siegel, Rachel. "Two Black Men Arrested at Starbucks Settle with Philadelphia for $1 Each." *Washington Post,* May 3, 2018.

Simmons, A. John. "Locke and the Right to Punish." *Philosophy and Public Affairs* 20, no. 4 (1991): 311–49.

Sitwell, William. "Dumplings and Vegan Double Acts: The Foodie Trends of 2018." *The Times,* online edition, Jan. 4, 2018.

"William Sitwell Meets the Woman Who Called Him Out for 'Vegan-Killing' Comments: This Time I'd 'Gone Too Far.'" *The Telegraph,* online edition, Jan. 27, 2019.

Smith, Adam. *Theory of Moral Sentiments.* New York: Penguin, 2010.

Springer, Elise. *Communicating Moral Concern: An Ethics of Critical Responsiveness.* Cambridge, MA: MIT Press, 2013.

Srinivasan, Amia. "The Aptness of Anger." *Journal of Political Philosophy* 26, no. 2 (2018): 123–44.

Strawson, P. F. "Freedom and Resentment." *Proceedings of the British Academy* 48 (1962): 187–211.

Swan, Sarah L. "Between Title IX and the Criminal Law: Bringing Tort Law to the Campus Sexual Assault Debate." *University of Kansas Law Review* 64, no. 4 (2016): 963–86.

Tadros, Victor. *The Ends of Harm: The Moral Foundations of Criminal Law.* New York: Oxford University Press, 2011.

Talbert, Matthew. "Moral Competence, Moral Blame, and Protest." *The Journal of Ethics* 16, no. 1 (2012): 89–109.

Teekah, Alyssa. "Lessons from Slutwalk: How Call-Out Culture Hurts Our Movement." *Herizons* (2015): 16–21.

Tosi, Justin, and Brandon Warmke. "Moral Grandstanding." *Philosophy and Public Affairs* 44, no. 3 (2016): 197–217.

Tunick, Mark. *Balancing Privacy and Free Speech: Unwanted Attention in the Age of Social Media*. New York: Routledge, 2015.

———. "Privacy and Punishment." *Social Theory and Practice* 39, no. 4 (2013): 643–68.

Twain, Mark. *The Adventures of Tom Sawyer*. Mineola, NY: Dover Publications, 1994.

von Hirsch, Andrew. *Censure and Sanctions*. New York: Oxford University Press, 1994.

"Waitrose Food: Editor William Sitwell Resigns Over 'Killing Vegans' Row." *BBC News*, online edition, Oct. 31, 2018.

"Waitrose Launches Massive New Range of 40 Vegan and Vegetarian Products," *Vegan Food & Living.com*, Oct. 10, 2018.

"Waitrose's Ex-'Killing Vegans' Editor Meets Vegan." *BBC News*, online edition, Nov. 26, 2018.

Waldron, Jeremy. "A Right to Do Wrong." *Ethics* 92, no. 1 (1981): 21–39.

Walker, Margaret Urban. *Moral Repair: Reconstructing Moral Relations after Wrongdoing*. New York: Cambridge University Press, 2006.

Weiner, Jonah. "Kevin Hart's Funny Business." *Rolling Stone*, online edition, July 29, 2015.

Wellman, Christopher Heath. "The Rights Forfeiture Theory of Punishment." *Ethics* 122, no. 2 (2012): 371–93.

Wertheimer, Roger. "Constraining Condemning." *Ethics* 108, no. 3 (1998): 489–501.

Wilk, Thomas. "Trust, Communities, and the Standing to Hold Accountable." *Kennedy Institute of Ethics Journal* 27, no. 2 (2017): 1–22.

Williams, Bernard. *Truth and Truthfulness: An Essay in Genealogy*. Princeton: Princeton University Press, 2002.

Williams, Garrath. "Sharing Responsibility and Holding Responsible." *Journal of Applied Philosophy* 30, no. 4 (2013): 351–64.

Wootson, Cleve R., Jr. "Add 'Performing Community Service while Black' to the List of Things That Make You Suspicious." *Washington Post*, May 15, 2018.

———. "A Black Yale Student Fell Asleep in Her Dorm's Common Room. A White Student Called Police." *Washington Post*, May 11, 2018.

———. "Police Say Woman Screamed Racial Slurs and Smacked a Black Teen at a Pool. She Lost Her Job." *Washington Post*, July 2, 2018.

———. "A White Woman Called Police on a Black 12-Year-Old – For Mowing Grass." *Washington Post*, June 30, 2018.

Wringe, Bill. *An Expressive Theory of Punishment*. Basingstoke, UK: Palgrave Macmillan, 2016.

Zaibert, Leo. "Punishment, Restitution, and the Marvelous Method of Directing the Intention." *Criminal Justice Ethics* 29, no. 1 (2010): 41–53.

———. *Punishment and Retribution*. New York: Routledge, 2006.

Index

For EU product safety concerns, contact us at Calle de José Abascal, 56–1°, 28003 Madrid, Spain or eugpsr@cambridge.org.

www.ingramcontent.com/pod-product-compliance
Ingram Content Group UK Ltd.
Pitfield, Milton Keynes, MK11 3LW, UK
UKHW020351140625

459647UK00020B/2398

*9 7 8 1 1 0 8 7 9 9 2 9 4 *